ROUTLEDGE LIBRARY EDITIONS:
LIBRARY AND INFORMATION SCIENCE

Volume 82

THE ROLE OF TRADE LITERATURE IN SCI-TECH LIBRARIES

THE ROLE OF TRADE LITERATURE IN SCI-TECH LIBRARIES

Edited by
ELLIS MOUNT

LONDON AND NEW YORK

First published in 1990 by The Haworth Press, Inc.

This edition first published in 2020
by Routledge
2 Park Square, Milton Park, Abingdon, Oxon OX14 4RN

and by Routledge
52 Vanderbilt Avenue, New York, NY 10017

Routledge is an imprint of the Taylor & Francis Group, an informa business

© 1990 The Haworth Press, Inc.

All rights reserved. No part of this book may be reprinted or reproduced or utilised in any form or by any electronic, mechanical, or other means, now known or hereafter invented, including photocopying and recording, or in any information storage or retrieval system, without permission in writing from the publishers.

Trademark notice: Product or corporate names may be trademarks or registered trademarks, and are used only for identification and explanation without intent to infringe.

British Library Cataloguing in Publication Data
A catalogue record for this book is available from the British Library

ISBN: 978-0-367-34616-4 (Set)
ISBN: 978-0-429-34352-0 (Set) (ebk)
ISBN: 978-0-367-36412-0 (Volume 82) (hbk)
ISBN: 978-0-367-36415-1 (Volume 82) (pbk)
ISBN: 978-0-429-34576-0 (Volume 82) (ebk)

Publisher's Note
The publisher has gone to great lengths to ensure the quality of this reprint but points out that some imperfections in the original copies may be apparent.

Disclaimer
The publisher has made every effort to trace copyright holders and would welcome correspondence from those they have been unable to trace.

The Role of Trade Literature in Sci-Tech Libraries

Ellis Mount
Editor

The Haworth Press
New York • London

The Role of Trade Literature in Sci-Tech Libraries has also been published as *Science & Technology Libraries*, Volume 10, Number 4, Summer 1990.

© 1990 by The Haworth Press, Inc. All rights reserved. No part of this work may be reproduced or utilized in any form or by any means, electronic or mechanical, including photocopying, microfilm, and recording, or by any information storage and retrieval system, without permission in writing from the publisher. Permission does not extend for any services providing photocopies for sale in any way. Printed in the United States of America.

The Haworth Press, Inc. 10 Alice Street, Binghamton, NY 13904-1580
EUROSPAN/Haworth, 3 Henrietta Street, London WC2E 8LU England

Library of Congress Cataloging-in-Publication Data

The Role of trade literature in sci-tech libraries / Ellis Mount, editor.
    p.   cm.
    "Also . . . published as Science & technology libraries, volume 10, number 4, summer 1990"—T.p. verso.
    Includes bibliographical references.
    ISBN 1-56024-038-5 (alk. paper)
    1. Libraries—Special collections—Catalogs, Commercial. 2. Catalogs, Commercial—Bibliography—Methodology. 3. Scientific libraries—Collection development. 4. Technical libraries—Collection development. 5. Libraries—Special collection—Commerce. 6. Commerce—Bibliography—Methodology. I. Mount, Ellis.
Z692.C36R64   1990
026.5—dc20
                                                    90-4806
                                                      CIP

The Role of Trade Literature in Sci-Tech Libraries

CONTENTS

Introduction	1
Online Vendor Library Index (OLVLI): A Unique System for the Management of Trade Literature at 3M *William T. Greene* *Larry K. Hoekstra* *Daniel J. Willis*	3
Background	3
Trade Literature Collection	4
Future Plans	8
Trade Catalogs in the Los Angeles Public Library *Billie M. Connor*	9
Historical Research in Trade Catalogs *Rhoda S. Ratner*	15
Value of Trade Catalogs	15
Major Collections	17
Library-Publisher Collaboration in the Preservation and Dissemination of Trade Catalogs *August A. Imholtz, Jr.* *Eric J. Massant*	23
Introduction	23
Providing Access to Trade Catalogs: Cataloging and Microfiche	24
Conclusion	29

Vendor Catalogs in Science/Technical Libraries: Why—and How   **31**
    Bruce Norton

  Product Catalogs—A Necessary Evil   31
  Vendor Catalogs in the Technical Library?   32
  How an IHS VSMF® Vendor Catalog System Works   32
  Indexing   33
  The IHS Solutions to Vendor Catalogs   34
  Full Catalog Services   34
  International (Non-U.S.) Catalog Services   38
  Side-by-Side Catalog Services   39
  IHS's Electronic Future in Catalog Services   40
  Science/Technical Libraries Need Vendor Catalogs   41

What Is *Thomas Register*?   **43**
    Rita Lieberman

SPECIAL PAPER

The Acquired Immune Deficiency Syndrome: A Bibliometric Analysis: 1980-1984   **45**
    Christopher D. Forney

  Chapter I: The Problem and Its Setting   46
  Chapter II: The Acquired Immune Deficiency Syndrome   49
  Chapter III: Review of the Related Literature   55
  Chapter IV: The Data and Their Treatment   59
  Chapter V: Results   61
  Chapter VI: Conclusions   67
  Acknowledgements   69

SCI TECH COLLECTIONS   91
    Tony Stankus, Editor

Brief Guide to Conservation Biology and Its Literature   **93**
    Ann Viera

  Introduction   93
  Overview of Conservation Biology   94
  Sources of Information   96

**NEW REFERENCE WORKS IN SCIENCE
    AND TECHNOLOGY**   **109**
        Arleen N. Somerville, Editor

SCI-TECH ONLINE   **125**
        Ellen Nagle, Editor

   Database News   125

SCI-TECH IN REVIEW   **131**
        Karla J. Pearce, Editor

Introduction

Many sci-tech librarians have had little or no experience with or knowledge of trade literature (often called manufacturers' catalogs). Yet this type of material plays a vital role in technology and the applied sciences. It provides data on the characteristics of a mammoth array of products and materials, data that are not often found in the conventional literature. Trade literature gives designers of products the type of information needed to make a decision as to whether or not to use a particular item. It also speeds up the design process. Trade catalogs are useful to purchasing agents, engineers, managers of factories and a wide range of other occupations.

Another value of this type of literature is its role in industrial history; old catalogs reveal a great deal of information about cultures and industries in other eras. Collections of older catalogs are being preserved in a more serious fashion now, including reprints of certain types.

This collection addresses all these aspects of trade literature including how they fit into library organizations. This latter topic is the theme of the first paper, written by William T. Greene, Larry K. Hoekstra and Daniel J. Willis. They describe how the 3M Corporation handles trade literature; a computerized system that was developed locally is fully explained. In the second paper Billie M. Connor reviews the role of trade catalogs over the years at the Los Angeles Public Library as well as the current collection management policy.

The next paper, by Rhoda S. Ratner, points out the different ways in which we benefit from a study of older catalogs; she also discusses catalogs that serve as indexes to major collections of such documents.

The fourth paper, which was written by August A. Imholtz, Jr., and Eric J. Massant, discusses major holdings of trade catalogs as well as projects for microfilming and cataloging important collec-

© 1990 by The Haworth Press, Inc. All rights reserved.

tions of such literature for preservation as well as sales purposes. In the next paper Bruce Norton describes the role played by Information Handling Services in providing libraries with up-to-date sets of trade catalogs in microfiche format, covering many subject disciplines. In addition the firm's online database is fully described. A brief description of the Thomas Publishing Company completes the papers on the theme.

The special paper for this book is an annotated bibliography, prepared by Christopher D. Forney, that is devoted to a survey of the literature on AIDS written during the period 1980-1984. He has analyzed citations in bibliographies published by the National Library of Medicine.

The special collection paper was written by Ann Viera on the topic of conservation biology and its literature. Important sources of information on the subject are also listed in this thorough analysis of a topic of global interest.

Ellis Mount
Editor

Online Vendor Library Index (OLVLI): A Unique System for the Management of Trade Literature at 3M

William T. Greene
Larry K. Hoekstra
Daniel J. Willis

SUMMARY. Providing information to clients in a thorough, timely and cost-effective manner is the established quality goal of 3M's Information Services department. The department consists of eight Technical Libraries, a Business Information Service, an Engineering and Vendor Library, a Patent and Technical Communication Service, a Current Awareness Service, and an Information Service Library in Austin, Texas.

This article will focus on a unique system developed by the Engineering and Vendor Library to collect, store, retrieve and disseminate trade literature. For this paper, trade literature is defined as product information from manufactures who provide goods and services to 3M. Being able to quickly retrieve this type of information is important, as it provides technical data and specifications used by laboratory, engineering, manufacturing and marketing personnel.

BACKGROUND

3M is a company of variety and versatility. The company manufactures and markets more than 50,000 products and services with operations in 52 countries. 3M has annual sales of over 10 billion

---

William T. Greene is Manager at 3M Company, Engineering and Vendor Library, 900 Bush Avenue, St. Paul, MN 55144. He has an MLS from Western Michigan University. Larry K. Hoekstra is Advanced Vendor Information Analyst at 3M Company, Engineering and Vendor Library. He received his MLS from the University of Minnesota. Daniel J. Willis is Senior Systems Analyst at 3M Company, Engineering and Vendor Library.

© 1990 by The Haworth Press, Inc. All rights reserved.

dollars and employs more than 82,000 people. The Information Services department at 3M is responsible for providing information support to 3M worldwide. It carries out this responsibility by collecting and developing information resources, providing ways of searching them (both manually and by computer) and by responding to requests for information. This article will describe a unique trade literature retrieval system that was developed by 3M's Engineering and Vendor Library to meet customer needs.

TRADE LITERATURE COLLECTION

A major objective of the Engineering and Vendor Library (E&VL) is to collect, store, retrieve, and disseminate trade literature. For this paper, trade literature is defined as product information from those manufacturers who provide goods and services to 3M. Engineers at 3M have long perceived the importance of being able to quickly retrieve product information from suppliers. From designing production equipment and specifying maintenance replacement parts, to upgrading manufacturing processes, engineers need to quickly identify product options and solutions.

The Engineering and Vendor Library's core collection of trade literature has been carefully selected and maintained, and presently consists of approximately 6,000 individual manufacturer's catalogs. This hard-copy collection serves as the primary trade literature resource. These catalogs represent the key manufacturers who provide goods and services to 3M, and are added to the collection only upon the recommendation of engineering or purchasing personnel. The library also subscribes to trade literature microfilm services which supplement the E&VL collection.

A detailed procedure for the acquisition of manufacturer's catalogs has been developed and is carefully followed. After the decision has been made to include a manufacturer in the collection, the process begins by identifying the local sales representative, who becomes an important part of the trade literature system. Personal contact is established with these sales representatives, and they are given detailed, written instructions on the standards to be met when submitting a catalog. The sales representatives are responsible for the preparation and upkeep of their catalogs. Standards require the local representative to supply a sturdy three ring binder to protect and organize the product literature; prepare a table of contents reflecting the alphabetical organization by manufacturer; and provide labeled tabs to allow easy location of literature within the binder. (See Figure 1.) These standards assure that the trade literature collection is neat, can stand up to heavy use, is well organized, and easy to use. In addition, the local sales representatives are asked to update their catalogs once a year, make all necessary additions or deletions and to prepare a new table of contents if necessary. Local sales representatives are very willing to spend time and effort in keeping their catalogs current as it is in their best interest to sell their products to 3M. Considerable staff time on the part of a Library Assistant is necessary to coordinate and supervise this process.

System Background

The initial index to the collection began as a 3 x 5 card file system for tracking manufacturers and their products. However it was difficult to continually add or change data on the cards and the

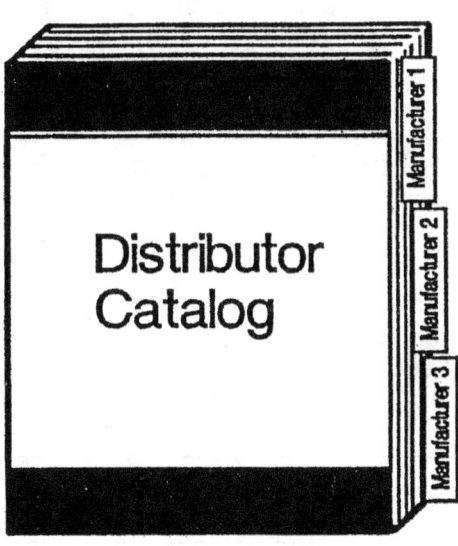

FIGURE 1

information could be accessed only by users in the library. The E&VL staff realized that a change from a card-based index to a computer-based index was essential. The perceived benefit would be an up-to-date service accessible from any 3M location worldwide.

In 1983, the card system was converted to a computer index using System 1022 database management software from Software House of Cambridge, MA. This system ran on Digital Equipment Corporation, (DEC) model 20 mainframes and was available to everyone on 3M's timesharing network. In 1987 the database was upgraded to System 1032 running on a DEC VAX 11/780 purchased by 3M's Information Services department. There are approximately 6,000 manufacturers, 15,000 product terms and 1,000 vendors or local representatives in the system.

Searching

Searching the system is very straightforward. The main menu allows searching by manufacturer name, by product, or by local representatives. (See Figure 2.) Approximately 70% of Online Vendor Library Index (OLVLI) users are looking for information on a manufacturer that they know by name. Searching consists of entering all or part of the name. OLVLI will then provide the company's

OnLine Vendor Library Index
[Search Via]
1- Manufacturer's Name 2- Product Term 3- Vendor or Distributor Name
Enter a Number > >

FIGURE 2

corporate address and phone numbers, including distributor information and the local sales representative. (See Figure 3.) A catalog number is listed for locating the shelf copy. Product and supplier searches work in a similar fashion in that a user simply needs to enter the general or popular name of the product or supplier. Many trade names have been included.

System Maintenance

The OLVLI system is maintained primarily by the Library Assistant and the Vendor Analyst. The Library Assistant is responsible for all data entry as well as coordinating new or updated information received from the local sales representatives. It warrants reemphasizing that frequent updating by sales personnel is a key element of maintaining current data in the catalogs. It is labor intensive but results in collection integrity.

The Vendor Analyst is then responsible for assessing the product literature in the catalogs and selecting product terms for the index. This review procedure continuously refines the index and prevents any duplication of product terms.

```
Machinery Manufacturing, Inc.
1467 Grand Boulevard
Forest Lawn, MI 60421
206/454-2030
```

Catalog	Distributor
41-LKH	LK Harvieux & Associates 612/778-4321 Contact: John Bryant
41-GRT	Great Northwest Representatives, Inc. 612/455-2340 Contact: George Jensen

```
Enter [Return] for menu > >
```

FIGURE 3

Customer Use and Access

Statistics indicate that 60% of OLVLI accesses are from remote users. The system is accessed 800 to 1,000 times per month, with the average customer performing 5 to 7 searches. The process is usually completed in less than two minutes from original login to logout.

Easy access to the system is available to any 3Mer who has use of a personal computer or terminal with a 3M network communications package. There is no charge to the user, as OLVLI resides on the Information Services department's mainframe computer. Ease of use is evident by the fact that during the five years that the system has been operational, there have been minimal complaints regarding use. The calls that are received are more of the type "I heard about your system, how can we connect?"

FUTURE PLANS

A number of future projects are planned for inclusion into the OLVLI system, including the incorporation of data from large scale information providers that currently produce their information in a text-only or a microfilm format. A system matching products with 3M Purchasing Agents is also planned. These enhancements will continue to make 3M's Online Vendor Library Index a system that saves considerable professional time in locating needed trade literature information.

Trade Catalogs in the Los Angeles Public Library

Billie M. Connor

SUMMARY. The history of Los Angeles Public Library's trade catalogs collection is described. Changes in selection criteria, organization and access over a seventy-five year period are reviewed. The resulting current collection management policy and its implementation are explained.

Los Angeles Public Library was established in 1872 to serve the City of Los Angeles. From its beginnings a strong Central Library collection was developed. Over time a branch and bookmobile service network evolved which now numbers sixty-three branches and two bookmobile units serving local communities within the City. In order to make specialized service available in specific areas of interest in the growing city, the Central Library established subject departments early in the twentieth century. As these special collections developed over the years, Los Angeles Public Library became the major public resource library for all of Southern California. It is now the collection used by the reference center of the Metropolitan Cooperative Library System, a consortium of libraries serving all of Los Angeles County (except the ninety-plus branches of a separate County library which belong to another consortium and which have no central library). Los Angeles Public Library houses the State of California Answering Network (SCAN), a statewide federally-funded third-level reference service, which also uses its collections

---

Billie M. Connor is Department Manager, Science, Technology and Patents, Los Angeles Public Library, 630 West Fifth Street, Los Angeles, CA 90071. The author holds a BS in education from Southwest Missouri State University, Springfield, MO and an MLS degree from Rutgers University.

© 1990 by The Haworth Press, Inc. All rights reserved.

as its primary resource. A large number of special libraries rely on it for supplementary materials and it is a resource for the area's academic libraries, particularly for general and trade literature.

Currently one of eleven subject departments in Central Library, the Science, Technology and Patents Department contains most of the trade catalogs owned by the Los Angeles Public Library. A selective collection of consumer mail order catalogs and directories of other available ones are in the Business and Economics Department. Portions of trade catalogs are included in the collections of other subject departments based on their subject areas. Some company catalogs of local historical importance are housed in the Rare Books and Special Collections Department.

Shortly after the establishment of the Industrial Department in 1914, later to become the Science, Technology and Patents Department, a trade catalogs collection was organized. Such a collection was found to contain much valuable information not only for current purchasing decisions but for historical data on specific products, industries, companies, prices and geographic areas. It also complemented the Library's patents and trademarks depository collection. Criteria developed for inclusion in the trade catalogs collection were: companies of local interest; those of regional or national prominence in an industry or trade; catalogs featuring products and services or industries significant in Southern California; and those on subjects important to other collection strengths; e.g., motor vehicles, etc. Catalogs were usually acquired by mailing list. Once received, they were indexed in-house in card files arranged by company name (with holdings) and a product, industry, and subject cross-reference file referring to company names. The catalogs were labeled and arranged by company name in folders in the closed stacks. Card files were publicly displayed in the reading room for library users to discover and/or librarians to use in answering reference questions. Individual catalogs or folders were retrieved by staff on request.

This method of organization and access was used for approximately seventy years with uneven success. Weeding was sporadic. Intermittently, the collection was not maintained well since each time staff workload required reduction because of vacancies, budgetary reductions of staff, etc., trade catalogs collection maintenance backlogs quickly developed since the catalogs were considered enrichment rather than basic sources. The usefulness of the collection naturally followed its state of maintenance.

When staff reductions came following California's passage of Proposition 13[1] in 1978, backlogs steadily built to the point that the decision had to be made to scale down the trade catalogs collection by reducing the number of companies represented. A form letter was sent to all companies no longer to be included in the collection requesting removal from their mailing lists. Over the following five years, backlogs were gradually worked through. In 1984, the collection development policy was reviewed for the Central Library as a whole and, with it, the component parts of every subject department. This reevaluation process produced the trade catalogs collection management policy that is followed at the present time.

The decision was made to reduce the historical collection to only those catalogs with state or local importance, with major significance to the history of technology (particularly if strong on illustrations), or those complementary to strong subject collections in the Library. Any catalog listed in Romaine's *A guide to American trade catalogs, 1744-1900*[2] was retained, as well. Those withdrawn from the collection were offered to dealers for credit if of any apparent value; if not, they were made available for sale at public book sales sponsored by the Department's community support "Friends" group. With the exception of one category, every catalog retained was fully cataloged and bound or otherwise suitably processed for shelving. "Automotive Ephemera," a special collection within the trade catalogs, was stored in file folders by make and year and within each make, by model. This file is now being entered into an in-house database using Inmagic[3] software. The latter collection includes media kits, glossy photographs, promotional brochures and other pieces related to the marketing of automobiles and trucks. Some of the pieces have become valuable as collectors' items and are housed in Special Collections. The file as a whole proves to be a useful adjunct to a strong motor vehicles collection.

Before the weeding and reorganization project was complete Los Angeles Public Library's Central Library experienced a disastrous fire on April 29, 1986. When the fire occurred, the trade catalog collection remaining to be reviewed was stored in a basement area separated from the fire. Water used by the firefighters to fight the blaze did not reach that section of the basement, either. Because of this isolation, the catalogs escaped the fate of most of the rest of the Science, Technology and Patents Department's collection, one-third of which was destroyed by fire and approximately one-half water-damaged. Flash freezing and later freeze-drying resulted in extensive salvage of that one-half although a considerable portion was not salvageable. The fortunate trade catalogs were packed out of the building immediately after the fire with the dry materials, sent for warehouse storage, and the review process was later completed in the warehouse. Those survivors now grace the shelves in the Central Library's temporary quarters where the Library reopened in May, 1989, and where public service will be given until the permanent building reopens in 1993 after expansion and renovation. During the post-fire recovery a new catalog was created with machine-readable records of all items inventoried after the fire and those cataloged in the interim. The cataloged trade catalogs now appear in the Library's CD-ROM catalog, or are in process and will appear on future disks.

Science, Technology and Patents' collection management policy now states: (1) collective trade catalogs are selectively acquired and retained; (2) a subscription is maintained to a current vendor catalog service kept up to date with replacement microfilm cartridges and accompanied by regularly updated indexes; (3) retrospective catalogs are selectively acquired, cataloged and retained based on geographic interest, significance of technology or company, and historical value to the collection; and (4) significant collections of historical trade catalogs published in microformat and marketed with printed guides are acquired as funds permit.

In the case of collective trade catalogs, such as *Sweet's*,[4] for example, space considerations have made selective retention decisions necessary. Such retention policy statements as "retain current and even-numbered years," or "retain current, previous and every five years," etc., are assigned to specific titles.

The current vendor catalog service on subscription is Information Handling Services' *Documentation service*,[5] which comes with indexes by vendor name, brand trade name, and product locator code. It is very expensive but offers unique information without labor intensiveness. New 16mm microfilm cartridges arrive as catalogs are added or replaced; superseded cartridges are sent back to the publisher. The Library plans to publicize this collection so that it will have sufficient use to warrant the cost.

Retrospective catalogs which would significantly enhance the local history collection are sometimes purchased from antiquarian booksellers and interesting donated ones are added if within the scope of the collection. No attempt is made to build an exhaustive historical collection since two Southern California academic institutions have important materials. The Library of the University of California, Los Angeles, includes some historical catalogs in its Special Collections Department. University of California, Santa Barbara, has the famous Romaine Collection of Nineteenth and Twentieth Century Trade Catalogs in its Library's Special Collections.

In recent years, various publishers have begun filming and marketing the contents of important historical trade catalog collections. Since Los Angeles Public Library's Central Library is the major urban resource library in Southern California, it has qualified for federal funds through the Major Urban Resource Library (MURL) program in each of the last several years. These funds are used to acquire materials to improve its collections in subject areas identified as critical needs by libraries in its service area. History of technology was added recently to the critical needs list. In 1989, a historical trade catalog collection published in microfiche format is being purchased with MURL funds, *Trade Catalogs from the Winterthur Museum.*[6] Similar acquisitions in coming years could enrich the Library's collection immensely.

The public library trade catalogs collection born in Los Angeles seventy-five years ago still thrives, interesting but different in appearance, content and character than it was in its early days. It has much in common with the City in which it exists.

NOTES

1. California. Constitution. *Constitution of the state of California as last amended November 8, 1988*; Article 13 A. *In* California. Assembly. *The Constitution* . . . Sacramento: California Legislature Assembly; 1989. 264p.

2. Romaine, Lawrence B. *A guide to American trade catalogs, 1744-1900*. N.Y.: R.R. Bowker; 1960. 422p.

3. *Inmagic*. Version: 7.1, release 1.0. Cambridge, MA: Inmagic, Inc.; 1988. [information retrieval/text indexing software package].

4. *Sweet's catalog file; products for general building and renovation*. Annual. N.Y.: Sweet's Group, McGraw-Hill Information Services Company; [one of several *Sweet's catalog files* published for the construction industry].

5. *Documentation service*. Englewood, Colorado: Information Handling Services; [current subscription service: vendor catalogs on microfilm; with 3-volume index listing in paper format].

6. *Trade catalogs from the Winterthur Museum*. Bethesda, MD: CIS Academic Editions; [microfiche, 3605 sheets: 14:1-24:1 reduction ratio; with companion printed guide, 438p.].

Historical Research in Trade Catalogs

Rhoda S. Ratner

SUMMARY. Trade catalogs document aspects of American history beyond the promotion of merchandise for sale. They have research value in material culture, graphic arts, printing history, labor conditions, cultural and social values, history of technology and the evolution of industries. Libraries are organizing their collections of trade catalogs and publishers are producing microformat editions. This article considers their availability, accessibility and preservation.

VALUE OF TRADE CATALOGS

Lawrence Romaine was a man with a mission. In 1960, when he published *A Guide to American Trade Catalogs, 1744-1900*, he was pleading his cause for the historical importance of trade catalogs. In his Introduction, he says, "It is high time that someone compiled and printed a record proving that Americans recognized the value of advertising catalogs and the mail order business even before they recognized the real value of freedom. There are ten thousand volumes that tell and retell the story of the American Revolution. I offer one that will, without bloodshed, convince you of the creative ability, imagination and Yankee ingenuity of the builders of this Republic throughout the 18th and 19th centuries."[1(p.ix)]

Romaine was a dealer, collector, and documenter of trade catalogs. In compiling the material for his book, he surveyed over 200 libraries, museums and historical societies, and too often received

---

Rhoda S. Ratner is Chief Librarian of the National Museum of American History Branch Library, Smithsonian Institution Libraries, Washington, DC 20560. She received her BA (Education) and MLS degrees at the University of Maryland.

© 1990 by The Haworth Press, Inc. All rights reserved.

responses that the collections were "stored in cases and trunks and have never been checked and cataloged" or were "set aside ready to catalog as soon as funds and staff can handle them." While he was grateful that libraries were taking this body of material seriously, he lamented the lack of funds for "the greatest panorama of industrial development ever printed."[1(p.x)]

His closing plea was, "If this volume encourages our library boards and 'angels' to recognize these invaluable records, and to provide funds and staffs to take care of them, not stored in boxes and cartons and trunks, unchecked, but rather properly cataloged and shelved where historians can find them, I shall feel amply paid for the time and effort that has gone into it."[1(p.xiv)]

Almost thirty years have passed and the prediction by A. Hyatt Mayer in the Foreword to the book proved accurate: "The new historians of business will find a basic tool in Mr. Romaine's bibliography of American catalogs, for it is the first general listing of these scarce ephemera in any country. Like any pioneer survey, its structure will always endure under the additions that the years must inevitably bring. Henceforth no American trade catalogue can be listed respectably without a Romaine reference, or boasting (while perhaps adding a penny to the price) 'Not in Romaine.' "[1(p.vii)]

In those same thirty years, there is ample evidence that trade catalogs are recognized as valuable research tools and that libraries are bringing them under control. Consider for a moment the levels of information that may be gained from a catalog:

- An item advertised in a catalog can represent the leap from patent dream to reality.
- During the last half of the nineteenth century, copy was often written by outstanding authors and historians, and embellished with woodcuts and lithographs executed by the best artists and engravers.
- An artifact will be fully documented as to size, materials and operation.
- Most catalogs will be dated. Some were deliberately undated to preserve the sense of currency. In those cases, the researcher may have the good fortune to be using a copy that was accessioned and date-stamped by a library shortly after publi-

cation. It would then be known that the object was produced before a certain date.
— Examples of printing history.
— The illustrations on the covers or within the catalog may represent the workplace, thus displaying labor conditions and procedures and perhaps even the function of tools — both their intended use and their place within a wider context.
— The items offered for sale are indicators of cultural values of the time and ideas about status — how people wished to see themselves.
— The catalog may serve to identify products that no longer exist.
— A series of catalogs can trace the history of technology and skilled workers and the evolution of industries.
— The prejudices of the time — ethnic, sexual or racial — may be demonstrated.
— The catalog may also document the shift of products from the elite to acceptance by the popular culture.

Glenn Porter, Director of the Hagley Museum and Library, summarizes the value of trade catalogs as follows:

> Trade catalogs open the doors to a wonderful world of instructive and fascinating things. They can help us to intuit much about the history of marketing and subtle shades of meaning in the material choices of our forebears. For students of those social systems, attitudes and values, and structures of meaning and symbol that constitute the realm of material culture, few printed forms of evidence are as richly rewarding, colorful, or interesting as the trade catalog.[2(p.13)]

MAJOR COLLECTIONS

Meanwhile, what have libraries been doing? In just the past few years, we have seen published guides to major collections at three institutions — Corning Museum of Glass,[3] Hagley Museum and Library,[2] and Winterthur.[4] While each of these libraries include what is generally defined as trade catalogs, there are some differences beyond the obvious.

In the broadest definition of the collection, Hagley terms trade catalogs as printed materials published by a manufacturing, wholesaling, or retailing firm to promote sales through advertising claims; instructions for using the product; testimonials from satisfied customers; and detailed descriptions of the products for sale. Nina de Angeli Walls adds that "although 'trade catalog' originally derived from the phrase 'to the trade,' referring to wholesalers and retailers only, the term now encompasses catalogs and circulars aimed at the ultimate consumer."[2(p.15)]

Corning includes design books, price lists, internal factory record books listing ware, and reprints, as well as trade catalogs that fit the standard definition. Winterthur includes broadsides, broadsheets, pamphlets, manuscripts, and books issued by businesses and individuals to entice the public to buy products.

Libraries have adopted cataloging methods appropriate to their own collections. Bibliographic access, however, beyond company name, is most often by subject. The sixty-two subject categories developed by Romaine for general collections have often been used and adapted to fit specific collections. In variations, the architectural trade catalogs in the Avery Library of Columbia University utilize Sweet's categories,[9] and the Smithsonian Institution Libraries use Library of Congress Subject Headings. Shelving arrangements run the full gamut. Catalogs may be arranged by subject, company name, accession number, or by call number when fully cataloged.

A researcher new to this body of literature is in luck if the name of the manufacturer is known. If only the artifact is at hand, however, there are means available to determine who produced what. To begin, Romaine and the three collection guides mentioned above may provide leads. An additional example of a subject-specific guide is *The finest instruments ever made: A bibliography of medical, dental, optical, and pharmaceutical company trade literature; 1700-1939* by Audrey B. Davis and Mark S. Dreyfuss.[5] Compared to Romaine's list of 250 medical and dental catalogs, this bibliography includes almost 10,000 citations for nearly 2,000 companies.

A librarian of an earlier time may also be of help. In 1934, the

Applied Science library at Columbia University was collecting current catalogs for use by the students. Once the catalogs were replaced by newer editions, single copies were kept for the historical collection. Granville Meixell, Librarian at the time, developed a manual with source lists for those attempting to build and organize such a collection. Her listing of Directories of Manufacturers was an aid in locating catalogs available in 1934. It is reproduced here to serve the present-day researcher as a guide to products produced in the past:[6(p.16)]

1. *Directory and Buyer's Guide* (Engineer (London, England))
2. *Engineering* (London) Directory
3. Federation of British Industries. *F. B. I. Register of British Manufacturers*
4. *Fraser's Canadian Trade Directory*
5. *MacRae's Blue Book*, consolidated with *Hendricks' Commercial Register of the United States for Buyers and Sellers*
6. *Thomas' Register of American Manufacturers and First Hands in all Lines*

When an object is not marked as to maker but is clearly identifiable as to type, U. S. Patents may be valuable sources of information. A cumulative index was published in 1873 covering the years 1790-1873 which can be searched by subject or inventor.[7] Following 1873, the annual reports of the U. S. Patent Office include the subject and inventor listings as well.

Since Romaine represents a first attempt at a union list of holdings, locating catalogs is often complicated. In Ash's *Subject Collections* there is a heading for Trade Catalogs—Collections; however the listing is not comprehensive.[8] Collections to be added are the Corning Museum of Glassware, Winterthur, the Athenaeum of Philadelphia (nineteenth-century house paint and lighting fixtures), the National Agricultural Library in Beltsville, Maryland (early American seed catalogs), and the Pennsylvania Horticultural Society (Pennsylvania seed catalogs). Historical societies and public libraries sometimes have collections of catalogs of products produced in their regions.

Trade catalogs are often treated as special collections, so the material is rarely available for loan. On-site use is usually possible, but there may be little opportunity for browsing. Dismal as the access picture may seem, it has considerably brightened recently with the advent of six collections in microformat.

1. Henry Francis du Pont Winterthur Museum.
Trade catalogues at Winterthur. New York:
Clearwater Publishing Co.
(UPA Academic Editions); [1984].

> Eighteen hundred catalogs arranged in 30 subject areas, with most of the catalogs dating from 1870 to 1910. A broad range of subjects including agricultural implements, clocks and watches, musical instruments, furniture, silver and clothing.

2. *Sweet's architectural trade catalog file*
Avery Library, Columbia University,
1906-1949. New York: Architectural Record Co.

> Each Sweet's volume consists of catalogs from hundreds of individual suppliers. The complete collection contains 2,334 microfiche.

3. *Architectural trade catalogs from Avery*
Library, Columbia University. New York:
Clearwater Publishing Co.
(UPA Academic Editions); [1988].

> One thousand six hundred and eighty-four catalogs covering 16 categories of building products organized in Sweet's catalog classifications.

4. Corning Museum of Glass. Library.
Trade catalogs. [Corning, N. Y.]: Corning
Museum of Glass, [1983].

> More than 2,300 foreign and domestic trade catalogs on glass products providing a primary source of information for study of the development of the glass industry throughout the world and the relationship of its products to the societies that created and used them.

5. Hagley Museum and Library. *Trade catalogs from the Hagley Museum and Library: Transportation*. Frederick, MD.: UPA Academic Editions; 1989.

> Some 1,000 catalogs dating from 1880 to 1940 including the following categories: Aircraft, automobiles, carriages and wagons, firefighting equipment and trucks, railroad equipment, and ships and boats.

6. Victoria and Albert Museum. *Trade catalogues in the Victoria & Albert Museum, London*. London, England: Mindata, 1986.

> Illustrated British and European trade catalogues dating from the late eighteenth century to the outbreak of the Second World War. The 322 microfiche are divided into three broad categories: Industrial/commercial, domestic and household, and fashion.

To the uninitiated, Romaine's enthusiasm about trade catalogs may seem excessive, and yet those of us who are keepers of collections share the enthusiasm. The Smithsonian Institution Libraries considers its trade literature collection as a national resource and a substantial proportion of its resources are allocated to bringing it under bibliographic control. As libraries prepare the materials, commercial publishers have demonstrated their willingness to film and make them available in microformat. This satisfies our common goals of preservation and access.

Taking preservation and access a step further, some libraries in the past have found that the trade catalogs in their holdings did not fit easily into their collections. The Smithsonian Institution Libraries has been the recipient of some gifts as a result, accepting the responsibility that comes with them. Other libraries have also made this commitment.

Thus, the message of this article is twofold. First, there are trade literature collections available to researchers in both hard copy and microformat. Suggestions have been provided on how and where to find them. Finally, readers are urged to consider their own collections. Are you holding uncataloged, unaccessible and perhaps fragile catalogs? Consider contacting one of the libraries who have made the commitment for their preservation and transferring the materials to them. Lawrence Romaine put his trust in us.

BIBLIOGRAPHY

1. Romaine, Lawrence B. *A guide to American trade catalogs; 1744-1900*. New York: Bowker; 1960.
2. Hagley Museum and Library. *Trade catalogs in the Hagley Museum and Library*. Wilmington, Delaware: Hagley Museum and Library; 1987.
3. Corning Museum of Glass. *Guide to trade catalogs from the Corning Museum of Glass*. New York: Clearwater Pub. Co., 1987.
4. Henry Francis du Pont Winterthur Museum. *Trade catalogues at Winterthur; a guide to the literature of merchandising, 1750-1980*. New York: Garland Pub., 1984.
5. Davis, Audrey B.; Dreyfuss, Mark S. *The finest instruments ever made; a bibliography of medical, dental, optical, and pharmaceutical company trade literature; 1700-1939*. Arlington, Massachusetts: Medical History Publishing Associates I; 1986.
6. Meixell, Granville. *The trade catalog collection; a manual with source lists*. New York: Special Libraries Association; 1934.
7. United States. Patent Office. *Subject-matter index of patents for inventions issued by the United States Patent Office from 1790 to 1873, inclusive*. New York: Arno Press; 1976.
8. Ash, Lee. *Subject collections; a guide to special book collections and subject emphases as reported by university, college, public, and special libraries and museums in the United States and Canada*. New York: Bowker; 1985.
9. McGraw-Hill Information Systems Company. Sweet's Division. *Sweet's catalog file. Products for general building and renovation*. NY: Sweet's Division, McGraw-Hill Information Systems Co., 1984.

Library-Publisher Collaboration in the Preservation and Dissemination of Trade Catalogs

August A. Imholtz, Jr.
Eric J. Massant

SUMMARY. Trade catalogs are an important historic record which have until recently been difficult to access in an organized fashion. Libraries have been collecting these ephemera, and have begun to catalog them. This, along with microfiche publishing, is providing broader and improved avenues to the promotional literature of the past for researchers in a variety of fields.

INTRODUCTION

Images of everyday life at the turn of the century; the latest in locomotive air-brake technology a hundred years ago; contemporary stationery, cutlery, musical instruments, toys, and cough medi-

---

August A. Imholtz, Jr. is Editor-in-Chief, University Publications of America, Academic Editions, 44 N. Market Street, Frederick, MD 21701. He received his BA in Classical Languages from Washington University and has completed all requirements except dissertation for a PhD in Classical Languages at The Johns Hopkins University. Eric J. Massant is Executive Editor, University Publications of America. He received his BS in Psychology from Old Dominion University and his MA in International Affairs from The American University.

The authors gratefully acknowledge the cooperation and assistance of those associated with the various projects mentioned in this paper—in particular, Norma H. P. Jenkins, Head Librarian at the Rakow Library, Corning Museum of Glass; Herbert Mitchell, Bibliographer at the Avery Library of Columbia University; Heddy A. Richter, Head of the Imprints Department at the Hagley Museum and Library; and Eleanor McD. Thompson, Librarian in Charge at the Henry Francis du Pont Winterthur Museum. Responsibility for any errors and the opinions contained in this piece remain with the authors.

© 1990 by The Haworth Press, Inc. All rights reserved.

cine in Boston in 1800. Trade catalogs depict these as no other historic record can. Although not meant to be a permanent chronicle, and few companies saved their older catalogs, thanks to the interest and foresight of collectors and librarians over the years these ephemera have been preserved. They can now be studied and enjoyed by social historians, art historians, archaeologists, historians of technology, and other academics, as well as non-academics such as hobbyists and renovators, restorers, and preservers of artifacts.

The principal purpose of trade catalogs was, of course, to promote the sale of the products listed therein. The practical and stylistic features of products are clearly evident in most catalogs. They not only describe the merchandise or service, but give us insight decades later into the values of the society and the context producers thought most appealing in which to present their goods. General examination of the changes in business and marketing strategies over the years can be made, as well as very specific observations on the development of advertising art in the promotional literature. Price lists in catalogs give us an economic perspective and provide opportunities for evaluating the consumer accessibility of goods in the society.

There currently exist a number of major trade catalog collections in the United States. Some cover a wide range of subjects and geographic areas while others focus on specific categories and localities. Many contain catalogs that are unique or nearly unavailable elsewhere. As important as these collections are, most have suffered from a major deficiency. Regional as well as nationwide access was until recently severely limited. Over the years, two approaches have been taken to remedy this situation.

PROVIDING ACCESS TO TRADE CATALOGS: CATALOGING AND MICROFICHE

Cataloging of trade catalogs was critical to providing access to this rich literature. Many collections are still not cataloged, or only partially cataloged. Those libraries that have taken the first important steps have followed various approaches, from cataloging on local card catalogs, through cataloging by Hollinger boxes containing multiple trade catalogs, to complete item-by-item cataloging, both of the latter on national cataloging utilities, the Research Libraries Information Network (RLIN) and the Online Computer Library Center (OCLC).

Although cataloging has clearly increased possible access by providing awareness of the material, researchers must still resort to travelling to the library holding the catalogs, or requesting them on inter-library loan. The latter option is often not available due to the rarity and fragility of these documents. Microfiche editions of the catalogs provide an efficient medium by which the volumes can be preserved and distributed while avoiding wear on the original materials.

Handling by researchers is not the only hazard suffered by these materials. For instance, in June 1972 tropical storm Agnes filled Corning's Rakow library with five and a half feet of water, severely damaging many of their trade catalogs. The catalogs were then frozen, to be thawed and cleaned later, a technique, incidentally, that bears some similarity to the initial restoration steps taken by the librarians of the Soviet Academy of Sciences Library in Leningrad after the disastrous February 1987 fire. Realizing the irreplaceable nature of this important collection of trade literature, the Rakow library began microfilming as part of its ongoing activities.[1]

Over the past few years, thousands of trade catalogs have been filmed. The Winterthur Museum, the Avery Library at Columbia University, the Corning Museum of Glass' Rakow Library, and the Hagley Museum and Library have major collections which are available on microfiche from University Publications of America in Frederick, Maryland. Some of these microfiche collections were enhanced by the inclusion of catalogs from other organizations.

Each institution focuses on certain broad categories. Winterthur on decorative arts, Avery on architecture, Corning on glass, and Hagley on industry and technology. Most of the catalogs promote American companies, with a few European, Russian, and Japanese catalogs included. The time spans range from the late eighteenth century to the mid-twentieth, covering the growth of industrialization and mass marketing in the United States.

Each collection has been divided into multiple classes. The classification of the Winterthur and Hagley collections evolved from

Lawrence Romaine's seminal work on trade catalog categorization, *Guide to American Trade Catalogs, 1744-1900*.[2] The Avery catalogs are organized according to a modified scheme suggested by the *Sweet's Architectural Trade Catalogs*. All of the collections were filmed by class, and within each class, alphabetically by company name, (the corporate author). The Corning collection, which contains the largest percentage of foreign catalogs, is also divided within each group into domestic and foreign sections. The 1906 through 1949 Sweet's Catalogs volumes, organized by year and category, were also filmed at Avery.

The microfiche publications are accompanied by printed guides which contain bibliographic information about each catalog. Catalog title, company location, publisher, date, collation, size, and, for the Avery and Winterthur collections, annotations are included. Dates will often appear in brackets, indicating that they were estimated. Many catalogs were published without dates, as they often are today, to maintain a perception of timeliness up until the next version of the catalog is published.

Subject and name indexing directs researchers to specific catalogs, with cross-referencing provided in many cases. The subject indexing is particularly important for catalogs that do not fall exactly into a specific category. Chronological and geographical indexes are also provided for most of the collections, enabling researchers to easily use additional avenues of access. Each guide is also prefaced by an introduction written by an authority on trade catalogs or the specific collection.

One of the first collections to be organized and fully cataloged was that of the Hagley Museum and Library. Over the years Hagley has collected approximately 20,000 catalogs focusing on industry and technology, the majority of which were published between 1880 and 1920.

In 1988, the Hagley Museum and Library entered into an agreement with the Academic Editions division of Congressional Information Service, later to become part of University Publications of America, a division of CIS, to film and market a selection of trade catalogs featuring the transportation trade.

The prior organization and cataloging by the library significantly facilitated the control of this project. A workable subset, transportation, was selected and the multiple cataloging approaches at Hagley simplified the preparation of the material for filming and the creation of the microfiche guide.

The Hagley collection had been organized into 58 categories. Six of these were selected for filming: *Aircraft; Automobiles; Carriages and Wagons; Fire Fighting Equipment, Fire Engines, and Trucks; Railroad Equipment and Supplies; and Ships and Boats.* A card catalog arranged by category and company simplified identification of the items to be filmed. However, these cards lacked the Library of Congress subject categories which did exist on the main library catalog.

Typically micropublishers prefer to have all materials sent to them for filming. UPA is no different, having a large filming operation with a proficient staff experienced with a wide variety of document types, from routine disposable reports to very fragile rare manuscripts. In addition, with the wide assortment of equipment available, all materials can be handled with optimal care, no matter what the size, color, or binding. Lastly, there is a greater degree of management oversight and control over the filming aspects of the project.

Libraries and owners of special collections, on the other hand, are sometimes very reluctant to part with their charges, or unable to do so because of a donor's stipulations that the materials not leave the library. Hagley required that the filming be done at their site. After sending a microfilm technician to review the materials to be filmed and identify the type of camera needed, UPA shipped and installed a camera at Hagley. The camera was set up in a special room with a high ceiling and light controls.

A camera operator was then sent by UPA to do the filming. Hagley's lovely institution and location on the banks of the Brandywine River helped alleviate somewhat the requirement to be away from home. The camera operator is one of the most significant contributors to the successful completion of any microfiche project. Not only do they have to be proficient at their craft, but they must also check for any errors, such as missing catalogs, inconsistencies in collection organization, and internal integrity of the documents themselves. Finally, as a salient link between the micropublisher and the institution, the camera operator must be able to deal in a pleasant and professional manner with the library personnel, as well as be sensitive to their concerns for the care of their documents.

Once a project is complete, the lasting impression made by the camera operator translates into a better relationship with the library community and ultimately into greater ease in finding and bringing to fruition new projects.

The catalog cards were pulled from the main catalog, in category-company order and copied front and back, to capture the subject terms. The trade catalogs to be filmed at Hagley were withdrawn from secure stacks and placed in the camera room. Several days of material were provided to prevent camera down-time. This reserve was maintained throughout the project, which took approximately a month to film. The card catalog copies were used to guide the camera operator in filming the trade catalogs in the correct order. A graduate intern at Hagley, working part-time, handled the copying of the cards and the procurement and organizing of the trade catalogs. This project gave the student the opportunity to work in his field while gaining some insight into the world of publishing.

Over one thousand catalogs were filmed at Hagley. The only items not pulled from the selected categories were those catalogs that had been reprinted by commercial publishers or had been copyrighted since 1960.

The card catalog copies were also used to create the guide to the microfiche. The data were entered on a word processor. Using database and typesetting software, the camera-ready copy of the guide was generated consisting of a bibliography and a name and subject index. The bibliography lists all the trade catalogs filmed by category (e.g., Automobiles), and within each group, alphabetically by company. A control number containing a code for each category was assigned to every catalog. For instance, all numbers for catalogs dealing with aircraft begin with "AI." This number appears in the bibliography, as well as on the eye-visible microfiche header.

Researchers might look up *Baldwin Locomotive Works* in the index, under which they would find 39 entries, ranging in date from 1881 to 1947. Each index entry is distinguished by the title of the catalog and the date. This saves the researcher time by assuring that only those catalogs that meet specific criteria need be reviewed. The control number is also listed, identifying the location of the catalog in the bibliography and in the microfiche collection.

The subjects provide pinpoint retrieval of catalogs. A search for catalogs covering *Steam Engines* yields references to six catalogs—

three in the Railroad section, two in Ships and one in Fire Engines. Someone could then compare the attributes of engines applied to different functions during the late 1800s.

Although UPA's guides to trade catalogs follow a fairly consistent format, with chronological and geographic indexes sometimes added, the production methods for different guides can vary significantly. In the case of the Hagley collection, we were fortunate to have a complete card catalog with Library of Congress subject terms. Other guides have been produced from straight keying into a database management system, with ultimate conversion into word processing software, for generation of camera-ready copy.

Another guide which proved relatively efficient to produce was for the *Trade Catalogs at Winterthur, Part 2.* The Henry Francis du Pont Winterthur Museum has an outstanding collection of decorative art trade catalogs which they have cataloged on OCLC. They provided UPA with the cataloging in machine-readable form, from which the guide to the microfiche collection was created.

CONCLUSION

Trade catalogs, like the earliest remnants of written Greek, the Mycenaean Linear B texts which are essentially records of inventories and accounts, provide the raw materials for quantifiable economic and historical research. Runs of company catalogs over years, or even decades in some cases, provide data series on the history of prices, data of increasing interest to economic historians. One can follow other changes of all sorts through the progression of trade catalogs. For example, as our nation's westward expansion progressed, centers of manufacture moved from the east coast to the midwest. Materials that were suited for life and work in New England were replaced with goods found to be necessary for life in the far west. This is true of the industrial catalogs, decorative catalogs, home furnishing catalogs, and catalogs of clothing and other items for personal consumption.

If the purpose of the trade catalogs was to market merchandise in the largest volume possible at the best possible price, the trade catalogs themselves have, however, become a unique record of technological development and manufacturing design in this country. Nor is the record one only of progress, for not all of the items depicted or listed in the trade catalogs have survived in private hands or even in public museums. As Lawrence Romaine in his pioneering work on trade catalogs observed in regard to a complete history of American manufacturers: "one good sixty-four page catalog with lithographed illustrations of a full line of products in any given field will, for such an undertaking, be worth seven tons of manuscript ledgers, day books, copy books, and correspondence."[3]

One can also find in these books, booklets, and brochures which were issued as catalogs much material for the analysis of the history of advertising and marketing. And then one can proceed to study what is signified, however latently, in many of the advertisements. For example, catalogs dealing with the clothing and the home can tell us much about class distinctions and role definitions for women. Architecture and furniture catalogs contain otherwise lost information for understanding how nineteenth century Americans defined themselves through building, room and space design, and furnishings.

The major collections of trade catalogs in this country, which were begun by private collectors and built up over the years, have now been acquired by libraries who face the responsibility of preserving the often fragile catalog record, making the record accessible through cataloging, and sharing this material itself with researchers. By joint ventures with a micropublisher it is possible for libraries and research institutions to achieve the goals of preservation and dissemination of materials that, though they were once tossed out with last year's almanac and other ephemera, can now tell us much more about our history than the price of cutlery and toys.

NOTES

1. The Corning Museum of Glass. *Guide to trade catalogs from the Corning Museum of Glass.* New York; 1987.

2. Nina Walls, *Trade catalogs in the Hagley Museum and Library,* Wilmington; 1987. Henry Francis du Pont Winterthur Museum. *Trade catalogues at Winterthur, a guide to the literature of merchandising, 1750 to 1980.* Edited by E. Richard McKinstry. New York: Garland; 1984.

3. Lawrence, Romaine, *A guide to American trade catalogs, 1744-1790,* New York: R. R. Bowker; 1960: p. xiv.

Vendor Catalogs in Science/Technical Libraries: Why — and How

Bruce Norton

SUMMARY. Science and technical libraries can perform a valuable service to engineers, parts specifiers, procurement agents, quality controls managers, and many others in their corporation by maintaining vendor catalog files on site. However, without proper file management, such collections can quickly become obsolete and incomplete. Information Handling Services (IHS) has been in the information management field for over 30 years, specializing in vendor catalog services in microform which are current, complete, and comprehensive. This article explores the range of services available from IHS and gives an overview of how these services can help the science/technical librarian more effectively meet clients' needs.

PRODUCT CATALOGS — A NECESSARY EVIL

An engineer attempts to check out specifications on a component needed for product design but can't find what he's looking for. He knows there must be several companies that manufacture the component, but his searches are futile. His associates try to help, but they can't find any information either. The engineer makes his way to the technical library.

The nightmare continues. In many instances, the engineer *and* the technical librarian find a few old data sheets after an exhaustive, involved search. The engineer asks the librarian to get the informa-

---

Bruce Norton is Director of Vendor Catalog Product Management for Information Handling Services. He has been with IHS for 15 years, and has been responsible for vendor products for over 7 years. Most recently, he has been instrumental in developing CD-ROM applications for IHS vendor catalog products.

© 1990 by The Haworth Press, Inc. All rights reserved.

tion for him—or he asks his secretary to send for it, which means the librarian once again is left with a collection of obsolete data pages of no use to anyone. And even if the librarian *does* secure the information, what then? In hard copy, chances are it will be gone—or torn apart—within a week or two.

VENDOR CATALOGS IN THE TECHNICAL LIBRARY?

Many librarians would respond, justifiably under the circumstances described above, that tracking product/vendor catalogs for engineers is a waste of time and effort, that keeping up with the hard copy is too difficult—updating is uncertain at best. Yet, there is a critical need to have this kind of information centralized in an area where many people can have easy access to it, in a format that prevents destruction or "permanent borrowing." Engineers and other users cannot possibly store in their offices all of the information on products that they need to have, so the library is the obvious location. And the library staff, if anyone, is trained to understand the need for currency and completeness and to respond to systems that provide those benefits. The combination of the location and training makes the science/technical library the ideal center for vendor catalog research.

HOW AN IHS VSMF® VENDOR CATALOG SYSTEM WORKS

Information Handling Services (IHS) has been producing industrial vendor catalogs on microfilm for over thirty years, and VSMF® (IHS's registered tradename for Visual Search Microfilm Files) has become a household word to most engineers and technical librarians. Why is the system so successful? For many reasons, among them frequency of updating and the level of indexing. Before IHS, there was no organized, consistent, or timely method of tracking catalog information. IHS not only microfilms every single page of a catalog, but indexes the information in a variety of ways and updates the file every sixty days as well. The microfilm format has an additional advantage—when the librarian or engineer locates the pages required, paper copies can be made and carried away from the file, leaving the original information intact in the proper place for the next user.

Currency and completeness are major issues, but equally important is comprehensiveness. IHS has a large data acquisition department, comprising many specialists whose sole responsibilities are tracking catalog updates, contacting manufacturers for new or revised information, and discovering other manufacturers who produce competing products. Thus, the IHS system automatically provides multiple sourcing for parts and components, allowing for the most comprehensive vendor information systems available.

IHS catalog services come in many configurations, from the Master Catalog Service complete database of over 25,000 vendors and nearly 100,000 catalogs, to specialized *Product Oriented Data Segments (PODS),* side-by-side comparisons of specific products. All of the services include comprehensive indexes.

INDEXING

Indexing is available in four ways:

- Vendor Name;
- Brand/Trade Name;
- Product/LOCATOR Code; and
- Federal Supply Class (FSC) Number.

Obviously, if you know the name of the vendor you're interested in, the alphabetic vendor name index is the first place to go. In the vendor name index, you'll find the primary name; divisional names; primary address; telephone numbers; cable, fax, TWX and telex numbers (when available); SIC and CAGE (Commercial and Government Entity) code numbers; and products manufactured/services provided, along with IHS microfilm/microfiche location. The brand/trade indexes also provide company names and film references.

The FSC (Federal Supply Classification) and Product/LOCATOR Code indexes are tied into the IHS LOCATOR Coding system, a unique classification scheme developed by IHS to logically identify groupings of products. The FSC index cross-references

FSC codes to the LOCATOR code, as does the product/subject index. Once the LOCATOR Code is known, the LOCATOR index can be used to identify vendors which produce a given type of product, making multiple sourcing easy and convenient.

THE IHS SOLUTIONS TO VENDOR CATALOGS

IHS provides its vendor catalog databases in a variety of logical arrangements, such as Full Catalog Services (including High Technology Services, Construction Services, Facilities Engineering and Maintenance Services, and Medical Services), International (non-U.S.) Catalog Services, and Side-by-Side Catalog Services. Each will be described in more depth below; each features high-quality indexing, currency, comprehensiveness and completeness.

FULL CATALOG SERVICES

The Full Catalog Services present the vendor catalogs alphabetically by vendor name, filmed cover to cover. Therefore, if you want to see the entire product listings or catalogs of a specific vendor, this is where you would find them. For easier searching, the Full Catalog Services have been divided as follows:

General Use Services

- Master Catalog Service—The entire database of vendor catalogs from over 25,000 industrial manufacturers, including drawings, schematics, specification sheets, applications data and pricing information. In addition, publications from over 200 associations, societies and institutes are provided.
- Distributor Catalog Service—Contains catalog data, product specifications, performance data, drawings and application notes from more than 1,200 distributors of commercial and industrial products.
- Vendor Oriented Data Segments (VODS)—Data modules containing product data and component data sheets. Groupings include such areas of specialization as electrical utility apparatus, electronic components, furniture/furnishings, lighting/

electrical wiring, engineering/testing equipment, fluid system components, and so forth.

High Technology Services

- Documentation Services — designed for purchasing, receiving/inspection, logistics, design, drafting and technical writing personnel who require OEM catalog or alternate source catalog data.
- Electro-Mechanical Catalog Service (EMCAT) — An information service for design, research, development and engineering fields with specific emphasis on electrical/electronic and mechanical components.
- Industrial Technology Service — Intended for the customer who requires original equipment manufacturer (OEM) data for industrial applications.
- INTEGRATED CIRCUIT PARAMETER RETRIEVAL® (ICPR®) Service — Contains characteristic data used in electronics design, purchasing, specifications, maintenance and other functions which require location and selection of integrated circuits.
- SEMICONDUCTOR PARAMETER RETRIEVAL® (SCPR®) Service — References characteristic data used in electronics design, specifications, maintenance, purchasing and other functions which require location and selection of discrete semiconductors and optoelectronic devices.
- Integrated Circuit Data Flash Service — An exclusive IHS product designed for specifiers who need current technical data on ICs and LSIs developed and manufactured in Japan.
- IC/SC EIA/JEDEC Reference Material — Contains publications and standards from the Electronics Industries Association (EIA) and the Joint Electronic Device Engineering Council (JEDEC) that are used with integrated circuits and discrete semiconductors.
- Component Information Systems Service — Vendor information for high technology design, research, development and engineering with specific emphasis on electrical/electronic components.

- HI-TECH 4 Service—Vendor data used for high technology research, development, and design engineering fields that require specific information on integrated circuits, semiconductors, passive devices and other electrical/electronic component parts.
- GML Information Service—Provides easily accessed comparative information on a wide range of computer equipment for use by all of industry and government agencies.

Construction Services

- AIA (American Institute of Architects) MASTERSPEC® Service—A vendor data information service for use by architects, engineers, interior developers, educators and students involved in the specifying process for building construction. Available in Architectural Structural/Civil and Mechanical/Electrical versions.
- Construction Catalog Service—Contains data pages from almost 5,000 vendors of commercial and industrial products/services including: construction/landscape equipment; building structural materials; lighting/electrical wiring; coatings/sealants/adhesives; and so forth.
- Construction Engineering Services—A combination service that contains elements from IHS's military, federal and vendor product lines, developed to meet specific military construction and engineering requirements.
- SPEC-DATA® II Building Products File—An information service developed jointly by IHS and the Construction Specifications Institute (CSI) utilizing the 16 Division Format of CSI's MP-2-1 MASTERFORMAT™.
- Construction Specification Service—A vendor information service that contains data required by architectural, facilities design, construction and maintenance operations in federal, state and city governments and the military. Includes the SPEC-DATA II information published by the Construction Specifications Institute.
- Government Architectural Engineering Service—A specialized combination product designed to meet the overall infor-

mation needs of large government organizations that require extensive construction/architecture systems.
- R.S. Means Building Construction Cost Data — Used by building professionals such as architects, design/construct contractors, real estate developers, corporate planners, appraisers and assessors who need rapid cost, budgeting, and estimating information for all levels of construction.

Facilities Engineering and Maintenance Services

- Plant Engineering Service — Product catalogs and technical data such as drawings, schematics, specification sheets, applications data and pricing information, provided on such subject areas as building mechanical equipment, CAD/CAM, chemicals/fuels/chemical products, cleaning equipment/supplies, electrical apparatus, and many, many more.
- Government Facilities Engineering System/Industry Facilities Engineering system — Combination information services designed for architects, facilities design, construction and maintenance operations in federal, state, and city governments and the military, containing SPEC-DATA II, R.S. Means, Plant Engineering Service, Federal Construction Regulations, selected ASTM, ASME, ANSI, AWS, AWWA, ACI, NEMA, and NFPA standards.

Medical Services

- Medical Equipment, Devices and Supplies (MEDS) Services — A vendor information service containing data required for effective performance by procurement, facilities engineering, supply, and other personnel involved in the identification and selection of medical supplies and equipment for health care facilities. Contains product specification sheets, performance data, drawings, schematics, pricing information and applications data on: medical distributors; furniture/furnishings; medical/dental equipment and supplies. Also includes the ECRI (Emergency Care Research Institute) *Health Devices Sourcebook*.

- Medical Requirements Group—A specialized combination product designed to meet the overall information needs of large medical facilities that require master systems of information; includes the MEDS Service above, plus the SOURCE ONE® Master GSA procurement service and the Veterans Affairs procurement service.

INTERNATIONAL (NON-U.S.) CATALOG SERVICES

- Canadian Catalog Service—Contains Canadian product catalog data covering all industries.
- UK Electronic Engineering Service—Comprises catalogs, product specifications and related technical information for manufacturers and suppliers of electronic equipment and components in the United Kingdom and from suppliers in other countries who have recognized agents or distributors in the United Kingdom.
- UK Engineering Components and Materials Service—Includes catalogs, product specifications and related technical information from manufacturers and suppliers of engineering components, materials and equipment including electrical, mechanical and electro-mechanical components.
- UK Process Engineering Service—Provides catalogs, product specifications and related technical information from manufacturers and suppliers of components and equipment for the processing and chemical engineering industry in the UK and from suppliers in other countries who have recognized agents or distributors in the UK.
- UK Laboratory Equipment Service—Contains catalogs, product specifications, and related technical information from manufacturers and suppliers of laboratory equipment, fittings, disposables, and all types of laboratory and analytical instrumentation used by research and laboratory areas in most industries and organizations.
- UK Manufacturing and Materials Handling Service—Contains catalogs, product specifications and related technical information from British manufacturers and suppliers of construction,

materials handling, packaging, air conditioning, and ventilation equipment, and manufacturing machinery.
- UK Construction and Civil Engineering Service—An information system developed to cover system responsibilities relating to plant construction and equipment, containing catalogs from British manufacturers and suppliers of building materials, equipment, services and components.
- Information Technology, Computer and Communications Hardware Index (ITCCHI)—An information service applicable to organizations involved in the design, development and procurement areas of aerospace, navigation equipment, radar and guidance systems, process control; communications networks; broadcasting; CAD/CAM/CAE systems design; computer turnkey systems, as well as government and commercial end-users of information technology equipment. Contains catalogs, brochures and product literature from British manufacturers and manufacturers who have UK agents.
- European Vendor Catalog Microfile—Product catalogs, specifications and related technical information from over 3,000 major European manufacturers of mechanical and electro-mechanical components.

SIDE-BY-SIDE CATALOG SERVICES

The Side-by-Side Vendor Catalog Services are arranged by product category. This arrangement allows for fast *comparative* searching of multiple vendor sources for specific products or components, since like items are arranged "side-by-side" in the file.

Product Comparison Services

- Design Engineering Service—A microfilm product that contains over 1,000,000 pages of component and product data sheets from more than 10,000 manufacturers. The data contained in this service includes catalog pages, product specifications, performance data, drawings, test data, applications data and related information. There are seven major product sections (Electrical, Electronic, Fluid Systems, Instruments, Ma-

terials and Fasteners, Power Transmission and Hardware, and Production Equipment and Services), which can be leased separately or in any combination.
- Metric Design Service—Includes metric-related component and product data sheets required for metric design and associated activities.
- Marine Engineering Service—Provides marine-related component and product data sheets. The information is used in marine engineering and marine industries such as shipbuilding, ship maintenance, and areas concentrating in vessel design, repair and overhaul.
- Product Oriented Data Segments (PODS)—Data modules which contain product and component data sheets specific to a certain product area. There are 67 modules representing such product groupings as actuators, air/water quality instruments, coatings/special compounds/fluids, dimensional measuring equipment, computer equipment, fibers/textiles/wood/pulp, and many, many more.
- *High Technology Services*—The side-by-side High Technology Services are covered under "Full Catalog Services." They include the INTEGRATED PARAMETER RETRIEVAL (ICPR), SEMICONDUCTOR PARAMETER RETRIEVAL (SCPR), Integrated Circuit Data Flash, Component Information System, and HI-TECH 4 Services.

IHS'S ELECTRONIC FUTURE IN CATALOG SERVICES

IHS introduced its first electronic vendor product in May 1989. The IC/Discrete Parameter Database Service on CD-ROM (Compact Disc—Read Only Memory), a MASTERNET™ Electronic Service, provides complete characteristic information on more than 880,000 active or discontinued commercial/military high reliability devices from more than 800 manufacturers worldwide. Recently, IHS added 277,000 raster-scanned manufacturer technical data pages to the database, providing *complete* accessibility to valuable, up-to-date electronic device information.

SCIENCE/TECHNICAL LIBRARIES NEED VENDOR CATALOGS

The truth is, engineers are paid to design products and systems, not to do research. The cost of an engineer's time to research products and services can be extremely expensive—especially if the search is unsuccessful. The less time an engineer has to spend in researching this information—and the more time he or she can spend in actually designing and implementing the project—the better it is for the entire company.

The science/technical librarian can provide a valuable service to the engineering staff by making current, complete, and comprehensive product and service information readily available and easily accessible. Not only will engineers benefit from this service, but so will many other people within the company—parts specifiers, procurement agents, and any others who need to know alternate source information.

An IHS vendor information system located in the science/technical library provides a resource which pays for itself continuously through saved time and, because of the wide range of vendors and products to select from, money too. In providing a service of this nature, the science/technical librarian enhances the library's status within the company and reinforces the worth of the library's services time and time again.

[Note: IHS, Information Handling Services, and VSMF® are registered trademarks of Information Handling Services. MASTERSPEC is a registered trademark of the American Institute of Architects. SPEC-DATA is a registered trademark of the Construction Specifications Institute. Registered U.S. Patent and Trademark Office. MASTERNET is a trademark of Information Handling Services. MASTERFORMAT is a trademark of the Construction Specifications Institute.]

What Is *Thomas Register*?

Rita Lieberman

SUMMARY. Briefly describes the contents of *Thomas Register of American Manufacturers*.

For over 60 years Thomas Publishing Company has concentrated its full energies on filling one of industry's greatest needs—the need for up-to-date product information. Today Thomas publishes seventeen major buying guides and eleven product news magazines.

Its largest publication, *Thomas Register of American Manufacturers*, is generally considered to be by far the most complete and helpful specifying and buying guide published today. This three-part system provides "instant" sourcing information for executives in purchasing, engineering, sales production, operations, research and development and marketing. The 1990 edition of *Thomas Register* has been expanded to include more than 1.75 million listings in the 23-volume directory.

The 14-volume Products and Services Section provides detailed information on the sources of nearly 52,000 industrial products and services. Each product or service heading is followed by a list of all known manufacturers or sources. Suppliers or sources are listed alphabetically by state and city within each state. The geographical arrangement enables users to locate vendors closest to the place where the material or product is needed. Supplementing these listings are informative advertisements with more details about the product or services.

There is a 2-volume Company Profiles Section which offers information about the capabilities and contact data on more than

---

Rita Lieberman is Promotion Manager, Thomas Publishing Company, One Penn Plaza, New York, NY 10001. She has a BA degree from Union College.

150,000 U.S. companies, listed alphabetically by company name. Many companies also provide a complete listing of their subsidiaries and divisions as well as their entire product line. In addition there is a trade or brand names index relating the names with the owner company. Identifying the source of a product known only by its brand name thus becomes a simple matter.

The 7-volume Catalog File Section provides over 10,000 pages of catalog data from more than 1500 companies. Catalogs are arranged alphabetically by company name; they are fully cross-referenced within both the Products and Services and Company Profiles sections. A reader seeing the referral line "See our Catalog in Catalog File Section" knows that it isn't necessary to call or write for a catalog since it is available in the Catalog Section with no further delay.

Evidence of the usefulness of the directory is found in the fact that 98% of the chief purchasing executives of Fortune 500 companies and 86% of the manufacturing firms listed on the New York Stock Exchange use *Thomas Register* to specify and buy products. Design, electrical and electronic engineers, purchasing agents, government buying at all levels and thousands of wholesalers, distributors and retailers consider it a mainstay of the workplace.

Further proof of its utility is seen in the fact that verified research shows that industry uses this directory in buying products and services at a rate of more than $400 million a day.

SPECIAL PAPER

The Acquired Immune Deficiency Syndrome: A Bibliometric Analysis: 1980-1984

Christopher D. Forney

SUMMARY. Citations from six bibliographies on the acquired immune deficiency syndrome (AIDS) for the years 1980-1984 were analyzed in order to provide some information on the journals in which articles on AIDS were published. A core list of eighteen journals was revealed.

Christopher D. Forney is Reference Librarian in the Fairfax County Library System's Special Services Department, 6209 Rose Hill Drive, Alexandria, VA 22310. He received the BS degree from Stephen F. Austin State University and the MLS degree from North Carolina Central University.

This paper was originally submitted to the faculty of the School of Library and Information Science, North Carolina Central University, in partial fulfillment of the requirements for the degree of Master of Library Science.

© 1990 by The Haworth Press, Inc. All rights reserved.

CHAPTER I
THE PROBLEM AND ITS SETTING

Statement of the Problem

Librarians may utilize several types of studies designed to assist them in determining the needs of their users: library surveys, user surveys, and bibliometric studies. The latter is a means of studying the various characteristics of a subject literature in a scientific manner in order to determine use patterns. These studies are unobtrusive and the measure of use may influence thinking on the structure of information and knowledge in that discipline, in addition to the formulation of collection development policies and practices.

To date, there has not been a bibliometric study of the acquired immune deficiency syndrome. Therefore, this study proposes to analyze the literature of the acquired immune deficiency syndrome in the journal literature. The study will determine the titles most frequently cited, the language in which papers are most frequently written, and the analysis of journals by country of publication.

The Hypotheses

The first hypothesis is that the majority of references will be written in English as opposed to a foreign language.

The second hypothesis is that the majority of journals will be published in the United States.

The third hypothesis is that there will be a core list of most frequently cited journals with information on AIDS.

The fourth hypothesis is that there will be no journals devoted solely to the acquired immune deficiency syndrome during the time period studied.

The Subproblems

The first subproblem is to determine in what languages the references were written. What is the percentage of references written in English compared to other languages?

The second subproblem is to determine the distribution of journals by country of publication. Will the majority of the journals be published in the United States?

The third subproblem is to rank the cited journal titles according to the frequency with which they are cited. Which titles constitute the core of most frequently cited periodicals?

The fourth subproblem is to determine if any journals devoted solely to AIDS exist. How many references were cited?

Delimitations

This investigation will be confined to references to articles on the acquired immune deficiency syndrome over the five-year period from 1980-1984. All references appeared in six National Library of Medicine bibliographies on AIDS. Analytical entries for annual reports, abstracts, bibliographies, conference and symposium proceedings, non-print materials such as video-recordings and cassettes, monographs, and other miscellaneous notes were excluded.

Definition of Terms

Citation. A citation is a bibliographic reference which is used to cite the authority for statements in the text. Citations may take the form of a footnote or a collection of references at the end of the paper.

Cited reference. The cited reference is the document to which the source article refers. In this study, the distribution of cited references by title and language serve as the basis for this investigation.

Citing reference. The citing reference is the source document of the citation. In this study, the database of citing references shall be composed of all source articles in the sample of bibliographies.

Core title. The core titles are the documents which receive the highest citation rate and, thus are the most important for that discipline.

Citation Rate. The citation rate is the number of times a publication has been cited. Citation rate in this investigation is calculated as the number of references to the acquired immune deficiency syndrome, discounting duplicate references to the same document.

Research Assumptions

The first assumption is that the selection of a paper for publication in a given journal indicates relevance of that material to the primary intended audience as judged by the editors. Relevance of the paper to readers outside of the intended discipline may be inferred from citation rate.

The second assumption is that there is a correlation between the citation rate and the importance of the journal, or group of journals.

Importance of the Study

The purpose of this bibliometric study is to give the working physician, researcher, and librarian an idea of where the literature on the acquired immune deficiency syndrome is located during the period from 1980-1984. The results of the study may be used as an acquisition tool for developing a journal collection on AIDS.

CHAPTER II

THE ACQUIRED IMMUNE DEFICIENCY SYNDROME

Background

Few diseases in modern times have raised such fears and uncertainties as the acquired immune deficiency syndrome, better known as AIDS, and the malignancies, infections, and brain damage that can accompany it. In a little more than eight years, AIDS has become a medical dilemma, literally wreaking a "viral war" upon a nation caught by surprise.[1] AIDS has grown from a clinical oddity to a virtual epidemic, half of whose victims have already expired and the vast majority of whom will be dead within three years of their seeking medical attention.

As of yet, there is no cure for AIDS, and both the layman and health professional face a medical challenge with uncertainty. The emergence of the acquired immune deficiency syndrome as a new and deadly catastrophe has been a grim reminder of the limitations of even the most advanced technology to respond to the onset of a medical crisis.[2]

Before it is over, countless individuals will be pushed to the limit in their quest for a solution to the AIDS epidemic. Physicians will become exasperated, while researchers remain perplexed by the plethora of clues. AIDS is burdening both the health care delivery system and society, and compounding everything is the revelation of certain segments of the population as the initial and principal victims of this medical phenomenon.[3]

At the same time, stunning successes in the sciences of epidemiology, virology, immunology, molecular biology, oncology, pharmacology, and pathology have led to discovery and description in intricate detail of the virus responsible for AIDS and the major pathways of its spread.[4] AIDS is a hot topic, an issue difficult to stay abreast of because of the non-stop media coverage which manages to outpace new developments of the disease itself. Critics, however, note that the information conveyed is often incomplete, taken out of context, tainted by social prejudice, or premature in inciting optimism.[5]

While researchers have determined those at risk of developing the disease, predicting the number of AIDS cases will be hard—the hardest of which concerns the future spread of the disease. Leading specialists estimate that 10% to 100% of those infected with the AIDS virus will eventually develop AIDS.[6] In the United States alone, an estimated 2.5 million Americans will be carriers of the virus by 1991. AIDS will be among the top ten leading causes of death, and the leading cause of death for people between the ages of 25 and 44 years.[7] Prominent AIDS researchers Robert Gallo and Emmanuel Heller comment on this devastating disease:

> The war on AIDS requires a global effort on the part of governments, multinational organizations, industry, scientists, public health workers, and educators. The virus is transmitted sexually and no one is immune. It is not confined to certain minorities of life style (drug addicts), sexual preference (homosexuals), or color, as the power and lability of human sexuality makes most of us susceptible and spread of the virus is an exponential process, giving the disease its relentless character and making the fight against it a race against time. If we make rapid and fundamental changes in our sexual behavior, we can, at least, slow its spread and buy time for the development of more effective drugs and a vaccine.[8]

Etiology

AIDS, an acronym for acquired immune deficiency syndrome, is a complicated disorder that hampers the defense system of the body.[9] Caused by a retrovirus,[10] victims of the disease fall prey to organisms that attack once healthy immune systems, thus making them prime targets for opportunistic infections not normally found in healthy people. The Centers for Disease Control (CDC), in Atlanta, Georgia, defines a person as having AIDS if one of the following fatal conditions is present: Kaposi's sarcoma (a tumor), Pneumocystis carinii pneumonia (a lung disease caused by a parasite), or a CDC identified list of other infections and conditions.

The AIDS virus may be contracted in one of two ways. First, a person can become infected by engaging in sex—oral, anal, vaginal—with someone who is infected with the AIDS virus. Second, one can become infected by sharing drug needles and syringes with an infected person. Those who get the AIDS virus may experience some or all of the following symptoms:

1. unexplained, persistent fatigue
2. unexplained fever, night sweats or shaking chills that last for several weeks or more
3. diarrhea that continues for several weeks
4. a dry cough that will not go away
5. purple or pink spots or bumps on or under the skin, inside the mouth, nose or around the eyes
6. white spots around or in the mouth that last for weeks

Many of these symptoms are similar to those of the common cold, the flu and other illnesses. The difference is the severity and the length of time that they last.[11] The name AIDS appropriately defines the condition. It is acquired, that is, not inherited but associated with the environment. Immune refers to the body's natural system of defense against disease, while deficiency indicates that the system is not functioning properly. Syndrome suggests that a group of particular signs and symptoms occur simultaneously and characterize a disorder.[12]

Epidemiology

The onset of the acquired immune deficiency syndrome leaped to the forefront of medical establishments in Spring 1981. Initially appearing in 1979, AIDS attracted the attention of the medical community when homosexual men began to develop unusual opportunistic infections. The infections proved to be fatal.[13] Observing this medical mystery was Dr. Michael S. Gottlieb and colleagues at the UCLA School of Medicine and Dr. I. Pozalski at Cedars Mt. Sinai Hospital in Los Angeles. Five young males were treated between October 1980 and May 1981 for pneumocystis carinii pneumonia (PCP), a rare infection. Other opportunistic infections were present and the citing of such disease alarmed the physicians. Reports of AIDS from the Centers for Disease Control, too indicated that pneumocystis carinii pneumonia and Kaposi's sarcoma (KS), a rare malignant tumor indigenous to equatorial Africa and highly prevalent in elderly men of Mediterranean or Jewish ancestry, signified that something was amiss and hinted to a new medical phenomenon.[14]

Individuals at Risk

Anyone can develop AIDS; that is, if exposed to infected blood or blood products. The epidemic, however, has been narrowed to the following individuals who are at a greater risk of acquiring the disease:

1. Homosexual or bisexual men
2. Intravenous drug abusers who share hypodermic needles
3. Hemophiliacs who have received infected blood products
4. Transfusion patients who have received infected blood products
5. Heterosexual partners of homosexual or bisexual men or those infected with the AIDS virus
6. Infants of parents with AIDS

Individuals infected with the virus can be classified into four general categories:

1. Asymptomatic carriers — healthy with no hints of immunosuppression or immune susceptibility
2. Persistent generalized lymphadenopathy (PGL) — well with glandular swellings (lymphadenopathy) in armpits, neck, and groin
3. AIDS-related complex (ARC) — impairment of the immune system along with fatigue, fever
4. Full-blown AIDS — symptomatic with life threatening opportunistic infections. It is the most severe of the stages of the human immunodeficiency virus. Death usually results.[15]

Many believe that the term AIDS has been misapplied to represent the entire spectrum of HIV diseases. AIDS is the end stage, the most devastating part of a wide range of HIV infections. Not everyone who is infected with the AIDS virus will develop AIDS. Individuals may not be affected by the virus immediately, for it may lie dormant for months or years before it manifests itself in the form of life-threatening infections, neurological disorders, and malignancies.[16]

Demographics of AIDS Victims

AIDS is believed to have originated on the African continent where the majority of its victims are heterosexual.[17] However, in the United States, the AIDS epidemic has been concentrated in specific areas. For the most part, many of the patients have been associated with metropolitan areas on both the east and west coasts, namely New York City, and California cities—San Francisco and Los Angeles, and Florida. The high rate of AIDS cases in urban America is probably attributed to the multitude of homosexuals residing in these cities and the fact that the "fast lane" lifestyle lived by these individuals greatly exposes the group to the disease. Homosexual and bisexual men, followed by intravenous (IV) drug users constitute the majority of AIDS cases reported in the United States.

Discovery of the AIDS Virus

The virus responsible for AIDS has had several names. Below are the former names of the virus and the term now used:

Names of the Virus

- Human T-Cell Lymphotropic Virus Type III (HTLV-III)
- Lymphadenopathy Associated Virus (LAV)
- AIDS Related Virus (ARV)
- Current Name: Human Immunodeficiency Virus (HIV)

Numerous research laboratories were involved in isolating the AIDS virus. As a consequence, a variety of names were given to the virus. Becoming the first to assign a name to the virus implied credit for isolating and characterizing the virus; honor, name recognition, increased research funds, secures power and increases the likelihood for scientific prizes. Moreover, the first to claim discovery of the virus would have an improved chance in obtaining the rights to patents and royalties stemming from the development of a test for the AIDS virus.

Three researchers take credit for discovering the virus linked to AIDS. In 1983, Barre-Sinoussi, Montagnier and co-workers at the Institute Pasteur in Paris, pinpointed the virus responsible for AIDS and named it lymphadenopathy-associated virus (LAV). Independent of the French researchers, Dr. Robert Gallo and fellow workers exposed the virus and termed it the human T-cell lymphotropic virus-III (HTLV-III). In San Francisco, an AIDS virus was isolated by Jay Levy and called AIDS-associated retrovirus (ARV). As of May 1986, the International Committee on the Taxonomy of Viruses suggested a new name for the retrovirus; human immunodeficiency virus would be the term used globally.[18]

NOTES

1. Blanchet, Kevin D. *AIDS: A health care management response*. Rockville, MD: Aspen Publications, Inc.; 1988; p. xi.
2. Mayer, Kenneth. *The AIDS Fact Book*. Toronto: Bantam Books; 1983. *passim*.
3. Fettner, Ann Guidici. The discovery of AIDS: perspectives from a medical journalist. In: *AIDS: acquired immune deficiency syndrome and other manifestations of the HIV infection*. Edited by Gary P. Wormser. Park Ridge, NJ: Noyes Publications; 1987; p. 2-3.
4. Bakerman, Seymour. *Understanding AIDS*. Greenville, NC: Interpretive Laboratory, Inc.; 1988; p. 1.
5. Gong, Victor. Facts and fallacies: an AIDS overview. In: *AIDS: facts and issues*. Edited by Victor Gong. New Brunswick, NJ: Rutgers University Press; 1987; p. 3.
6. Daniels, Victor G. *A.I.D.S. the acquired immune deficiency syndrome*. Hingham, MA: MTP Press; 1987; p. 1-3.
7. Bakerman. *Understanding AIDS*; p. 3.
8. Gallo, Robert C. Foreword to *AIDS: acquired immune deficiency syndrome and other manifestations of the HIV infection*. Edited by Gary P. Wormser. Park Ridge, NJ: Noyes Publications; 1987; p. ix.
9. Daniels. *A.I.D.S.* p. x.
10. Bakerman. *Understanding AIDS*. p. 3.
11. Harris County Medical Society and Houston Academy of Medicine. *AIDS: a guide for survival*. Houston: Harris County Medical Society; 1987; p. 13.
12. Gong. Facts and Fallacies. *AIDS: facts and issues*; p. 4.
13. Daniels. *A.I.D.S.* p. 1.
14. Choi, Keehan. Assembling the AIDS puzzle: epidemiology. In: *AIDS: acquired immune deficiency syndrome and other manifestations of HIV infection*. Edited by Gary P. Wormser. Park Ridge, NJ: Noyes Publications; 1982; p. 15.
15. Gong. Facts and fallacies. *AIDS; Facts and issues*; p. 11.
16. Langione, John. *AIDS: the facts*. Boston: Little Brown; 1988; p. 4.
17. Bakerman. *Understanding AIDS*; p. 10.
18. Ibid., 1.

CHAPTER III
REVIEW OF THE RELATED LITERATURE

The term bibliometrics may be used generically to describe a series of techniques that seek to quantify the process of written communication.[1] The techniques date back to the efforts of early twentieth century documentalists who applied mathematical and statistical analysis to bibliographic units.[2]

Pritchard[3] coined the term bibliometrics in 1969. Previously used was the term "statistical bibliography" which was introduced by Hulme in 1923. Hulme defined statistical bibliography as the "illumination of the processes of sciences and technology by means of counting documents."[4] Because the term was used little in the literature and subject to misinterpretation, Pritchard suggested that the term bibliometrics be used in which he defined as "the application of mathematics and statistical methods to books and other media of communication."[5] The term proved favorable and has been used in the literature ever since.

Raisig, in an essay on the health sciences, provided a more exact and practical definition of bibliometrics (which in 1962 was still called statistical bibliography):

> the assembling and interpretation of statistics relating to books and periodicals . . . to demonstrate historical movements, to determine national or universal research use of books and journals, and to ascertain in many local situations the general use of books and journals.[6]

Hawkins describes bibliometrics in a recent definition as "the quantitative analysis of the bibliographic features of a body of literature."[7] It is in this sense that the term is now used.

Bibliometric studies and research may be classified in a variety of ways. One way would be by the types of data on which the studies are based and another by the purpose or application of the studies. Two principal methods used to examine the literature in a specific subject field are the citation-counting method and the analysis of entries listed in a bibliography or appropriate abstracting or indexing service.[8]

The citation-counting method, which is also known as citation analysis, is a bibliometric technique used to determine the number of citations received by a given document or set of documents over a period of time from a particular set of citing documents.[9] The citations are usually found at the end of articles or are footnotes within the articles. Works used in preparation of, or having made a contribution to the source paper characterize the true citation analysis.[10]

Gross and Gross conducted the first citation analysis in 1927 in an attempt to identify journal titles indispensable in chemistry. Using a single volume from *The Journal of the American Chemical Society*, 3633 references were found to be distributed among 247 titles. The leading 28 journals were identified and arranged in order of the number of references.[11] Coile[12] and Meadows[13] used this method to rank the journals in electrical engineering and astronomical literature. Sengupta,[14] using the citation-counting method, ranked one hundred and sixty-five journal titles in the field of physiology which he thought served as the "medium for dissemination of physiological knowledge."

Use of the citation-counting method for studying the characteristics of the periodical literature of a field must be used with care. For example, a significant portion of what is published and read may never be cited. Moreover, because of self-citing among journals, the results tend to depend on which journals are chosen. Self-citing was greater than 80 percent in each of the source journals according to Lawani in Cave's[15] study of tropical agricultural literature.

Another method used to study the periodical literature of subject field is the analysis of entries in a bibliography or abstracting or indexing service appropriate to one's area of inquiry.[16] Of the two approaches, this method is believed to be the most comprehensive and least biased when studying the use and characteristics of the literature in a particular field.[17] In his study of the broad field of science and technology, Martyn[18] discovered that roughly 79 percent of the published papers were covered in appropriate abstracting services. Papers not included showed no sign of being lesser in quality or value; however, editorial bias influenced what materials would be included. Editorial bias aside, results based on this method would be more representative of the total literature than those based on citation analysis.[19]

The earliest bibliometric studies were based on bibliographies. Cole and Eales[20] in 1917 conducted a statistical analysis on the literature of comparative anatomy from 1543 to 1860. The duo simply counted the number of titles, both book and journal articles, grouped them by country, within periods, and by division of animal world. Hulme's[21] investigation of the journal entries in "English International Catalogue of Scientific Literature" yielded four important tables:

1. the rank order of entries in physiology, bacteriology, serology, and biology
2. the rank order of sciences based upon their output of periodical literature
3. the number of journals referred to in the annual issues arranged by subject
4. the number of indexed journals arranged by countries

Lawani[22] studied the periodical literature of tropical and subtropical agriculture in 1972 in an attempt to shed light on the periodicals in which articles on tropical and subtropical agriculture appeared. A ranking of the periodicals and an analysis by language were also presented.

Brennen and Davey[23] in 1978, performed a similar study when they analyzed citations indexed in *Tropical Diseases Bulletin*, the only abstracting service exclusively devoted to tropical medicine. Their investigation during the period 1972-1975 analyzed every article indexed in forty-eight issues of *Tropical Diseases Bulletin* by the journal in which they were published and the language in which they appeared. Six hundred and forty-one (641) titles were identified with 41 journal titles providing 53.7 percent coverage of the periodical literature in the field.

NOTES

1. Ikpaahindi, Linus. An overview of bibliometrics: its measurements, laws, and their applications. *Libri*. 35: 1985 June; p. 163-167.

2. White, Emile C. Bibliometrics: from curiosity to convention. *Special Libraries*. 76; 35-42; 1985 Winter.

3. Pritchard, Alan. Statistical bibliography or bibliometrics? *Journal of Documentation*. 24 (4): 348-349; 1969.

4. Hulme, E. W. *Statistical bibliography in relation to the growth of modern civilization*. London: Grafton; 1923. 44p. Cited by Pritchard, p. 348.
5. Pritchard. *Statistical bibliography*. p. 349.
6. Raisig, L. M. Statistical bibliography in the health science. *Bulletin of the Medical Library Association*. 50: 450-461; 1962 July. Cited by S. M. Lawani. Bibliometrics: foundations, methods, and applications. *Libri*. 31: 294-315; 1981.
7. Hawkins, Donald T. Unconventional uses of on-line information retrieval systems. On-line bibliometric studies. *Journal of the American Society for Information Science*. 28:(1): 13-18; 1977.
8. Brennen, Patrick W. Citation analysis in the literature of tropical medicine. *Bulletin of the Medical Library Association*. 66:(10): 24-29; 1978.
9. Smith, Linda C. Citation analysis. *Library Trends*. 30: 83-106; 1981 Summer.
10. Broadus, Robert N. The application of citation analysis to collection building. *Advances in Librarianship*. 7:299-335; 1977.
11. Gross, L. K. College libraries and chemical education. *Science*. 66: 385-389; 1929 October 28.
12. Coile, C. Periodical literature for electrical engineers. *Journal of Documentation*. 8(4):209-226; 1952 Dec. Cited by S. W. Lawani. Periodical literature of tropical and subtropical agriculture. *UNESCO Bulletin for libraries*. 26(2):88-93; 1972 March-April.
13. Meadows, A. J. The citation characteristics of astronomical research literature. *Journal of Documentation*. 23(1):28-33; 1967 March.
14. Sengupta, N. Recent growth of the literature of biochemistry and changes in ranking of periodicals. *Journal of Documentation*. 29(2):192-211; 1973.
15. Cave, Roderick. Tropical agriculture literature citations. *Quarterly Bulletin*. (International Association of Agricultural Librarians). Doc. 8: 163-169; 1963 July. Cited by Lawani, Periodical literature, p. 88.
16. Brennen. Tropical Medicine. p. 25.
17. Lawani. Tropical and subtropical agriculture. p. 89.
18. Martyn, John. Tests on abstracts journals. *Journal of Documentation*. 23 (1): 45-70; 1967 March. Cited by Lawani, p. 89.
19. Lawani. p. 90.
20. Cole, F. J. The history of comparative anatomy, Part I. A statistical analysis of the literature. *Science Progress*. 11:578-596; 1917 April.
21. Hulme. Growth of modern civilization. Cited by Ikpaahindi. p. 163.
22. Lawani. p. 88-93.
23. Brennen. p. 25-29.

CHAPTER IV
THE DATA AND THEIR TREATMENT

The Data

The database for this study consists of references to the acquired immune deficiency syndrome gathered from references to articles published over the five-year period from 1980-1984 in bibliographies produced by the National Library of Medicine. The bibliographies, initially prepared by Charlotte Kenton, now a retired NLM librarian, consist of articles on AIDS that were chosen from approximately 3000 English and foreign language journals and monographs. These journal and monograph articles appear in *Index Medicus* and other bibliographies produced by NLM. References in the bibliographies were retrieved from NLM's MEDLINE database. In addition, a supplement found at the end of each bibliography contains the following: citations from journals received daily by the Library, citations to abstracts, monographs in press, and bibliographies. According to the compiler, "the bibliography covers citations to the current epidemic of serious illnesses associated with defects in the body's immune system."[1]

Admissibility of the Data

Data was collected only from citations which included all bibliographic elements relevant to this study: title and language. Titles were confirmed by checking reference sources such as *Index Medicus*, *Ulrich's International Periodical Directory*, and the National Library of Medicine's CATLINE database. Since the data was collected at NLM, the National Institutes of Health Library (NIH), and the McKeldin Library at the University of Maryland, College Park, which are major research libraries with substantial holdings, it was often possible to find the items in question in the library.

The Research Methodology

This study covered a five-year period, January 1980 to December 1984, and included every reference to an article in six bibliographies on the acquired immune deficiency syndrome. The references were analyzed according to the journals in which they appeared and the languages in which they were published.

Treatment of Each Subproblem

Subproblem One

The data needed to determine the percentage of the total citations which were in the English language were the total number of references and the number which were written in English. The data were collected on a data collection sheet and the percentage calculated.

Subproblem Two

The data needed to determine the percentage of the total journals published in the United States were the total number of journals and the number that were published in the United States. The data were collected on a data collection sheet and the percentage calculated.

Subproblem Three

The data needed to rank the most frequently cited titles are their respective citation rates. Those titles receiving twenty or more citations were sorted by descending numerical order. The titles on this list are the "core" documents for the acquired immune deficiency syndrome.

Subproblem Four

The data needed to identify the number of references found in a journal title specifically devoted to AIDS is obtained by locating the journal title and noting the number of times each journal was cited and recorded thus in the times cited column.

NOTE

1. Keaton, Charlotte. *National Library of Medicine Literature Search: The acquired immune deficiency syndrome No. 83-1.* Bethesda, MD: Government Printing office; 1985; p. i.

CHAPTER V
RESULTS

There were a total of 2122 articles analyzed in 420 periodical titles in this study. Four titles changed names during the course of the study; therefore, they were counted only once. Thus, the number of periodical titles for this study consist of 416 titles. The results of the analysis by language are shown in Table 1. Data in Table 2 contain the results of the analysis by country of publication. The core titles appear in Table 3. A complete listing of the journals in rank order during the five-year period from 1980-1984 appears as an appendix.

Results of Subproblem One

Hypothesis one stated that the majority of papers would be in the English language. This proved to be correct. The analysis by language in Table 1 indicates that English is by far the most important language in the literature of the acquired immune deficiency syndrome. English accounts for 337 titles with 1931 articles, for a total of 90.99 percent of all papers. Of all papers, 9 percent are in languages other than English. German, French, Spanish, and Dutch with contributions to the total literature of 2.26 percent, 1.89 percent, 1.46 percent, and 1.04 percent respectively are the other main languages in which articles on AIDS are published. The other languages in which papers are published are Japanese, Swedish, Danish, Czech, Norwegian, Italian, Portuguese, Russian, Hebrew, Hungarian, Chinese, Finnish, Serbo-Croatian, Rumanian, Polish, Slovak, and Turkish.

Results of Subproblem Two

Table 2 shows the distribution of journals by country of publication. The United States and the United Kingdom lead, followed by France, Switzerland, West Germany, Denmark, Canada, Japan, and Italy. However, 63.22 percent of the journals in the list are published in the United States, and only 7.45 percent are published in the United Kingdom. The results support the hypothesis that the majority of the journals would be published in the United States.

TABLE I

ANALYSIS OF LANGUAGE OF THE JOURNAL LITERATURE OF THE ACQUIRED IMMUNE DEFICIENCY SYNDROME

LANGUAGE	NUMBER OF PERIODICAL TITLES	NUMBER OF PAPERS	PERCENTAGE OF ALL PAPERS
English	337	1931	90.99%
German	17	48	2.26%
French	23	40	1.89%
Spanish	8	31	1.46%
Dutch	3	22	1.04%
Japanese	6	9	0.42%
Swedish	1	9	0.42%
Danish	2	7	0.33%
Czech	1	3	0.14%
Norwegian	3	3	0.14%
Italian	3	3	0.14%
Portuguese	1	3	0.14%
Russian	2	2	0.09%
Hebrew	1	2	0.09%
Hungarian	1	2	0.09%
Chinese	1	1	0.05%
Finnish	1	1	0.05%
Serbo-Croatian	1	1	0.05%
Rumanian	1	1	0.05%
Polish	1	1	0.05%
Slovak	1	1	0.05%
Turkish	1	1	0.05%
Total	416	2122	100%

TABLE 2

ANALYSIS OF JOURNALS BY COUNTRY OF PUBLICATION

COUNTRY OF PUBLICATION	TOTAL NUMBER OF JOURNALS PUBLISHED	PERCENTAGE OF TOTAL JOURNALS
United States	263	63.22%
United Kingdom	31	7.45%
France	16	3.85%
Switzerland	15	3.61%
West Germany	14	3.37%
Denmark	11	2.64%
Canada	7	1.68%
Japan	7	1.68%
Italy	5	1.20%
Belgium	3	0.72%
Norway	3	0.72%
The Netherlands	3	0.72%
Spain	3	0.72%
Australia	3	0.72%
Sweden	3	0.72%
New Zealand	2	0.48%
Ireland	2	0.48%
Czechoslovakia	2	0.48%

TABLE 2 (continued)

Mexico	2	0.48%
Finland	2	0.48%
East Germany	2	0.48%
Russia	2	0.48%
Brazil	1	0.24%
Chile	1	0.24%
Hungary	1	0.24%
Israel	1	0.24%
Argentina	1	0.24%
Jamaica	1	0.24%
Zimbabwe	1	0.24%
Puerto Rico	1	0.24%
Poland	1	0.24%
Rumania	1	0.24%
China	1	0.24%
Yugoslavia	1	0.24%
South Africa	1	0.24%
Turkey	1	0.24%
Unknown	1	0.24%
Total	416	100%

TABLE 3

CORE LIST OF JOURNAL TITLES

RANK	JOURNAL TITLE	NO. TIMES CITED
1	Lancet	246
2	New England Journal of Medicine	163
3	Annals of Internal Medicine	134
4	JAMA	87
5	Clinical Research	57
6	Journal of Cell Biochemistry, Supplement	49
7	Science	45
8	Morbidity and Monthly Weekly Report	45
9	Nature	41
10	British Medical Journal	32
11	Proceedings of the American Society of Clinical Oncology	32
12	American Journal of Clinical Pathology	26
13	Canadian Medical Association Journal	25
14	Journal of Infectious Diseases	25
15	Pediatric Research	25
16	Laboratory Investigation	24
17	American Journal of Medicine	24
18	Federation Proceedings	23

Results of Subproblem Three

The third hypothesis, that there would be a core list of journals is supported by the findings of this study. Eighteen journals produced twenty citations or more. The list in Table 3 depicts the core journals in descending order by citation rate. The most important titles in the literature are *Lancet, The New England Journal of Medicine, Annals of Internal Medicine, The Journal of the American Medical Association, Clinical Research,* and *The Journal of Cell Biochemis-*

try, Supplement. Of the eighteen titles listed in rank order of productivity, all were published in English. These eighteen titles accounted for 52 percent of the total literature covered during the period of the study. A most important fact based on the data in this study is that relatively few journal titles are required if a library wished to have adequate coverage of the acquired immune deficiency syndrome.

Results of Subproblem Four

One journal title devoted specifically to AIDS surfaced. *AIDS Research*, a U.S. publication, yielded 14 citations during the five-year study. According to the editor, the journal is a "critical journal that provides an essential forum for basic research and clinical observations on Acquired Immunodeficiency Syndrome."[1]

Sengupta[2] noted during his investigation of the literature in biochemistry that journals begin to emerge once that branch of scientific knowledge gains recognition as a distinctive discipline. As a result, a rise in the number of periodicals will reflect the growth of the specialized area of knowledge. The growth usually takes place in three steps:

1. increase in size of established periodicals
2. establishment of new periodicals for publication of research results from new geographical areas where interest in the new branch has become widespread
3. establishment of new journals to cover special areas of the scientific discipline which assume importance as a result of increasing specialization

NOTES

1. Bolognesi, Dani, ed. *AIDS research*. 1(1): x; 1983.
2. Sengupta, N. Growth of the literature of biochemistry. *Journal of Documentation*; p. 193.

CHAPTER VI
CONCLUSIONS

The present bibliometric analysis of the acquired immune deficiency syndrome from 1980-1984 provides information useful to librarians for preparing or managing a collection of materials geared to the special needs of the AIDS researcher.

Four hypotheses were posed at the outset of this investigation. It is now possible to determine if the hypotheses were correct based on the data collected and analyzed.

The first hypothesis indicated that the bulk of references would be written in the English language. This was clearly confirmed. 90.99 percent of all papers were written in English.

The second hypothesis stated that the majority of journals would be published in the United States. Again, this proved to be correct. More than half, or 63.22 percent of the journals were published in the United States.

The third hypothesis revealed a core list of most frequently cited journals. Eighteen journals with twenty or more citations on AIDS surfaced. These eighteen titles accounted for 52 percent of the total literature covered during the period of the study. The most important titles in the literature were *Lancet*, *The New England Journal of Medicine*, *Annals of Internal Medicine*, *The Journal of the American Medical Association (JAMA)*, *Clinical Research*, and *The Journal of Cell Biochemistry, Supplement*.

The fourth hypothesis stated that no journals exclusively devoted to AIDS existed before 1984 or during the course of this investigation. This proved to be incorrect. One title, *AIDS Research*, appeared among the 416 titles. The journal yielded fourteen citations during the five-year study.

BIBLIOGRAPHY

Bakerman, Seymour. *Understanding AIDS*. Greenville, NC: Interpretive Press; 1988.

Blanchet, Kevin D. *AIDS: A health care management response*. Rockville, MD: Aspen Publications, Inc.; 1988.

Bolognesi, Dani, ed. *AIDS research*. New York: Mary Ann Liebert, Inc.; 1983.

Brennen, Patrick W. Citation analysis in the literature of tropical medicine. *Bulletin of the Medical Library Association*. 66(10):24-29; 1978.

Broadus, Robert N. The application of citation analysis to collection building. *Advances in Librarianship*. 7: 299-355; 1977.

Cave, Roderick. Tropical agriculture literature citations. *Quarterly Bulletin*. 8:163-169; 1963 July.

Choi, Keenhan. Assembling the AIDS puzzle: epidemiology. In: AIDS: *Acquired immune deficiency syndrome and other manifestations of the HIV infection*. Ed. by Gary Wormser. Park Ridge, NJ: Noyes Publications; 1982.

Coile, R. C. Periodical literature for electrical engineers. *Journal of Documentation*. 8(4): 209-226; 1952.

Cole, F. J. The history of comparative anatomy. Part I: a statistical analysis of the literature. *Science Progress*. 11: 578-596; 1971 April.

Daniels, Victor G. *A.I.D.S. The acquired immune deficiency syndrome*. Hingham, MA: MTP Press; 1987.

Fettner, Ann Givdici. The discovery of AIDS: perspectives from a medical journalist. In: *AIDS: Acquired immune deficiency syndrome and other manifestations of the HIV infection*. Ed. by Gary Wormser. Park Ridge, NJ: Noyes Publications; 1987; p. 2-3.

Gallo, Robert C.; Heller, Emmanual. Foreword to *AIDS: Acquired immune deficiency syndrome and other manifestations of the HIV infection*. Edited by Gary Wormser. Park Ridge, NJ: Noyes Publications; 1987.

Gong, Victor. Facts and fallacies: an AIDS overview. In: *AIDS: facts and issues*. New Brunswick, NJ: Rutgers University Press; 1987.

Gross, P. L. K.; Gross, E. M. College libraries and chemical education. *Science*. 66: 385-389; 1929 Oct. 23.

Harris County Medical Society and Houston Academy of Science. *AIDS: a guide for survival*. Houston: Harris County Medical Society; 1987.

Hawkins, Donald T. Unconventional uses of on-line information retrieval systems: on-line bibliometric studies. *Journal of the American Society for Information Science*. 28(1): 13-18; 1977.

Hulme, E. W. *Statistical bibliography in relation to the growth of modern civilization*. London: Grafton; 1923.

Ikpaahindi, Linus. An overview of bibliometrics: its measurements, laws and their applications. *Libri*. 35:163-177; 1985 June.

Kenton, Charlotte. *National Library of Medicine literature search: the acquired immune deficiency syndrome*. 83-1; 1985.

Langione, John. *AIDS: the facts*. Boston: Little Brown; 1988.

Lawani, S. W. Periodical literature of tropical and subtropical agriculture. *UNESCO Bulletin for Libraries*. 26: 88-93; 1972; March-April.

Martyn, John. Tests on abstracts journals. *Journal of Documentation*. 23: 45-70; 1967 March.

Mayer, Kenneth. *The AIDS fact book*. Toronto: Bentam Books; 1983.

Meadows, A. J. The citation characteristics of astronomical research literature. *Journal of Documentation*. 23(4): 348-349; 1972.

Pritchard, Alan. Statistical bibliography of bibliometrics. *Journal of Documentation*. 25(4): 348-349; 1969.
Raisig, L. M. Statistical bibliography in the health sciences. *Bulletin of the Medical Library Association*. 50: 450-461; 1962 July.
Sengupta, I. N. Recent growth of the literature of biochemistry and changes in ranking of periodicals. *Journal of Documentation*. 23: 28-33; 1967 March.
Smith, Linda C. Citation analysis. *Library Trends*. 30: 83-106; 1981 Summer.
Turabian, Kate L. *A manual for writers of term papers, theses and dissertations*. 5th ed. Chicago: University of Chicago Press; 1987.
Ulrich's international periodicals dictionary. 27th ed. NY: Bowker; 1988.
White, Emile C. Bibliometrics: from curiosity to convention. *Special Libraries*. 76; 35-42; 1985 Winter.

ACKNOWLEDGEMENTS

The author would like to take this opportunity to thank Dr. Robert M. Ballard, my advisor, but foremost, mentor during my course of study at North Carolina Central University. You have fueled my desire to explore and to accomplish all that I desire to. Many thanks to the staffs at the Oregon Health Sciences University, the National Library of Medicine and the National Institutes of Health Library for their assistance.

APPENDIX

List of journal titles on the acquired immune deficiency syndrome--arranged in rank order

RANK	TITLE OF JOURNAL	NUMBER OF ARTICLES
1	Lancet	246
2	New England Journal of Medicine	163
3	Annals of Internal Medicine	134
4	Journal of the American Medical Association (JAMA)	87
5	Clinical Research	57
6	Journal of Cellular Biochemistry (Supplement)	49
7	Science	45
8	Morbidity and Monthly Weekly Report (MMWR)	45
9	Nature	41
10	British Medical Journal	32
11	Proceedings of the American Society of Clinical Oncology	32
12	American Journal of Clinical Pathology	26
13	Canadian Medical Association Journal	25
14	Journal of Infectious Diseases	25
15	Pediatric Research	25
16	Laboratory Investigation	24
17	American Journal of Medicine	24
18	Federation Proceedings	23
19	Ned Tijdschr Geneeskd	19
*20	European Journal of Clinical Microbiology	19

*Asterisk indicates journals that have changed titles, merged, or are obsolete during the course of this study.

21	American Journal of Roentgenology	16
22	Gastroenterology	16
23	Antibiotics and Chemotherapy	16
24	American Review of Respiratory Disease	14
25	Archives of Internal Medicine	14
26	Medicina Clinica	14
27	Radiology	14
28	AIDS Research	14
*29	Topics in Clinical Nursing (Current Title: Holistic Nursing Practice)	13
30	Southern Medical Journal	13
31	Public Health Reports	12
32	Hospital Practice	12
33	Seminars in Oncology	11
*34	British Journal of Venereal Diseases (Current Title: Genitourinary Medicine)	11
35	Medical Journal of Australia	11
*36	Scandinavian Journal of Haematology, Supplementum (Current Title: European Journal of Haematology Supplementum)	10
37	Chest	10
*38	Presse Medicale (Current Title: La Presse Medicale)	10
39	Archives of Pathology and Laboratory Medicine	10
40	Human Pathology	9

APPENDIX (continued)

RANK	TITLE OF JOURNAL	NUMBER OF ARTICLES
41	Larkartidningen	9
42	Hospitals	9
43	Journal of Pediatrics	9
44	MMW	9
45	Critical Care Medicine	8
46	American Journal of Ophthalmology	7
47	Journal of Clinical Investigation	7
48	Annals of Allergy	7
49	Journal of Allergy and Clinical Immunology	7
50	Neurology	7
51	Clinical and Experimental Immunology	6
52	Wisconsin Medical Journal	6
53	Journal of Clinical Immunology	6
54	Deutsche Medizinische Wochenschrift	6
*55	Western Journal of Medicine	6
56	Ugeskrift for Laeger	6
57	American Academy of Dermatology. Journal	6
58	Schweizerische Medizinische Wochenschrift	5
59	Ophthalmology	5
60	Postgraduate Medicine	5

61	Clinical Immunology and Immunopathology	5
62	Archives of Ophthalmology	5
63	Infection Control	5
64	Boletin - Asociacian Medica de Puerto Rico	5
65	Zeitschrift Fuer Hautkrankheiten H Und G	5
66	Sangre	4
67	Progress in Clinical and Biological Research	4
68	Klinische Wochenschrift	4
69	New Zealand Medical Journal	4
70	American Journal of Public Health	4
71	North Carolina Medical Journal	4
72	American Dental Association. Journal	4
73	Archives of Neurology	4
74	Cutis	4
75	American Journal of Pathology	4
76	Blood	4
77	Oral Surgery, Oral Medicine and Oral Pathology	4
78	Pediatrics	4
79	South African Medical Journal	4
80	Hastings Center Report	4

APPENDIX (continued)

RANK	TITLE OF JOURNAL	NUMBER OF ARTICLES
81	American Journal of Epidemiology	4
82	Cancer	4
83	American Journal of Nursing	4
84	American Family Physician	4
85	Praxis Und Klinik der Pneumologie	3
86	Medical Clinics of North America	3
*87	Arizona Medicine (Merged with Western Journal of Medicine)	3
88	California Dental Association. Journal	3
89	Journal of Clinical Microbiology	3
90	British Journal of Ophthalmology	3
91	Archives of Otolaryngology (Current Title: Archives of Otolaryngology - Head and Neck Surgery)	3
92	Florida Medical Association. Journal	3
93	Annales de Dermatologie et de Venereologie	3
94	American Journal of Gastroenterology	3
95	Vox Sanguinis	3
96	National Academy of Sciences of the United States of America. Proceedings	3
97	Gastro-Enterologie Clinique et Biologique	3
98	Mount Sinai Journal of Medicine	3
99	Connecticut Medicine	3
100	Journal of the American Osteopathic Association	3

101	National Cancer Institute. Journal (JNCI)	3
102	American Journal of Obstetrics and Gynecology	3
103	American Association of Cancer Research. Proceedings	3
104	Disease - A - Month	3
105	Journal of Neurosurgery	3
106	California Nurse	3
107	Revista Paulista de Medicina	3
108	Sexually Transmitted Diseases	3
109	Hospital Practice [Office Edition]	3
110	Medical Hypotheses	3
111	Ophthalmology	3
112	American Journal of Infection Control	3
113	Progress in Medical Virology	3
114	European Journal of Cancer and Clinical Oncology	3
115	Vasa	3
116	Journal of Clinical Gastroenterology	3
117	Diagnostic Microbiology and Infection Disease	2
118	European Journal of Respiratory Disease (Supplement)	2
119	New Zealand Nursing Journal	2
120	IRB: A Review of Human Subjects Research	2

APPENDIX (continued)

RANK	TITLE OF JOURNAL	NUMBER OF ARTICLES
121	Circulation	2
122	Cancer Investigation	2
123	Journal of Investigative Dermatology	2
124	General Dentistry	2
125	Oncology Nursing Forum	2
126	Archives d'Anatomie et de Cytologie Pathologiques	2
127	Boletin Col Prof Enterm	2
128	Blut	2
129	New York State Journal of Medicine	2
130	Rinsho Byori	2
131	Reviews of Infectious Diseases	2
132	Surveys of Immunology Research	2
133	Digestive Diseases and Sciences	2
134	Birth Defects	2
135	Revista Medica de Chile	2
136	Scandinavian Journal of Infectious Diseases	2
137	Laboratory Animal Science	2
138	Home Health Journal	2
139	Niedersachs Zahnarztebl	2
140	Diseases of the Colon and Rectum	2

141	Nippon Rinsho	2
142	Ohio State Medical Journal	2
143	Psychosomatics	2
144	Revue Francaise de Transfusion et Immuno - Hematologie	2
145	Orvosi Hetilap	2
146	Tijdschrift voor Ziekenverpleging	2
147	Urologic Clinics of North America	2
148	Annales de Pathologie	2
149	Colorado Medicine	2
150	Clinical Journal	2
151	Journal of Oral and Maxillofacial Surgery	2
152	Annals of Surgery	2
153	Obstetrics and Gynecology	2
154	Hepatology	2
155	Infection	2
156	Thrombosis and Haemostasis	2
157	Harefuah	2
158	Laryngoscope	2
159	ZFA. Zeitschrift for Alternsforschung	2
160	American Pharmacy	2

APPENDIX (continued)

RANK	TITLE OF JOURNAL	NUMBER OF ARTICLES
161	Home Healthcare Nurse	2
162	Advances in Experimental Medicine and Biology	2
163	Journal of Emergency Nursing (JEN)	2
164	Offentliche Gesundheitswesen	2
165	Medicina	2
166	American Journal of Tropical Medicine and Hygiene	2
167	Acta Neuropathologica	2
168	Medical Letter on Drugs and Therapeutics	2
*169	Schweizerische Rundschau Fur Medizin Praxis	2
170	Journal of Practical Nursing	2
171	West Indian Medical Journal	2
*172	Canadian Nurse - L'Infirmiere Canadienne	2
173	Comprehensive Therapy	2
174	Irish Medical Therapy	2
175	Dermatologic Clinics	2
176	Postgraduate Medical Journal	2
177	Seminars in Roentgenology	2
178	Texas Medicine	2
179	Casopis Lekaru Ceskych	2
180	Hautartz	2

181	Yale Journal of Biology and Medicine	2
182	American Journal of Diseases of Children	2
183	British Dental Journal	2
184	Acta Clinica Belgica	2
185	Internist	2
186	Journal of Dermatologic Surgery and Oncology	2
*187	Nursing Times (Current Title: Nursing Time, Nursing Mirror)	2
*188	Nouve Presse Medicale (Current Title: La Presse Medicale)	2
189	Clinical Nuclear Medicine	2
190	Journal of Clinical and Laboratory Immunology	2
*191	Kango (Current Title: Nursing/Kango)	2
*192	Nursing Mirror (Current Title: Nursing Times, Nursing Mirror)	2
193	Nurse Practitioner	2
194	FDA Drug Bulletin	2
195	Growth	2
196	Critical Care Update	2
197	Transfusion	2
198	American Journal of the Medical Sciences	2
199	Medical Society of New Jersey. Journal (Current Title: New Jersey Medicine)	2
200	Research Resources Reporter	2

APPENDIX (continued)

RANK	TITLE OF JOURNAL	NUMBER OF ARTICLES
201	Anesthesiology	2
202	Irish Journal of Medical Science	2
203	PRAXIS	2
204	Vnitrni Lekarstvi	2
205	RN	2
206	Cancer Treatment Report	2
207	Archives of Dermatology	2
208	Cancer Research	2
209	Medicine	2
210	Journal of Cellular Biochemistry	1
211	Archives of Andrology	1
212	Health Care	1
213	Cell and Tissue Kinetics	1
214	Journal of Pathology	1
215	Journal of the American College of Cardiology	1
216	Journal of Infection	1
217	Union Medicale du Canada	1
218	Journal of Clinical Pathology	1
219	CRC Critical Reviews in Immunology	1
220	Journal of the Royal Society of Medicine	1

221	Australian and New Zealand Journal of Medicine	1
*222	Kango Gijutsu (Current Title: Japanese Journal of Nursing Arts)	1
223	Bulletin of the World Health Organization	1
224	Hematological Oncology	1
225	Revue Medicale de Bruxelles	1
226	Revue de L'Infirmiere	1
227	Red Med Inst. Mex Seguro Soc.	1
228	Clinical Engineering Information Service	1
229	Experimental Hematology	1
230	Respiratory Care	1
231	Kansas Medical Society. Journal (Current Title: Kansas Medicine)	1
232	Journal of Submicroscopic Cytology	1
233	Australian Dental Journal	1
234	Wien Klinische Wochenschrift	1
235	Journal of Chronic Diseases	1
236	Journal of Neuro-Oncology	1
237	Journal of Immunology	1
238	Journal of Laboratory and Clinical Medicine	1
239	Infection and Immunity	1
240	Duodecim	1

APPENDIX (continued)

RANK	TITLE OF JOURNAL	NUMBER OF ARTICLES
241	Biochemical and Biophysical Research Communications	1
242	Transactions of the American Clinical and Climatological Association	1
243	Journal of Hospital Infection	1
244	Pathology Annual	1
245	Tandlaegebladet	1
246	Dermatologische Monatsschrift	1
247	Pennsylvania Dental Journal	1
248	CRC Critical Reviews in Clinical Laboratory Sciences	1
249	Ear, Nose, and Throat Journal	1
250	Arizona Nurse	1
251	Przeglad Dermatologiczny	1
252	International Dental Journal	1
253	Michigan Dental Association. Journal	1
254	Transplantation Proceedings	1
255	Otolaryngology - Head and Neck Surgery	1
256	Cancer Nursing	1
*257	International Journal of Oral Surgery (Current Title: International Journal of Oral and Maxillofacial Surgery)	1
258	Annals of Ophthalmology	1
259	Acta Ophthalmologica	1
260	Comprehensive Psychiatry	1

261	Journal of Biological Response Modifiers	1
262	Virchows Archiv. A, Pathological Anatomy and Histopathology	1
263	Cancer Immunology, Immunotherapy	1
264	American Journal of Hematology	1
265	Medecine Tropicale	1
266	Dermatologica	1
267	Rhode Island Dental Association. Journal	1
268	Dimensions of Critical Care Nursing	1
269	Michigan Medicine	1
270	Soins	1
271	Clinical Nephrology	1
272	Clinics in Haematology	1
273	Missouri Medicine	1
274	Archives of Neurology	1
275	West Virginia Medical Journal	1
276	Sykepleien	1
277	Rev Ig [Bacterial]	1
278	Tsa Chih	1
279	British Journal of Hospital Medicine	1
280	Central African Journal of Medicine	1

APPENDIX (continued)

RANK	TITLE OF JOURNAL	NUMBER OF ARTICLES
281	Illinois Dental Journal	1
*282	American Journal of Medical Technology (Current Title: Journal of Medical Technology)	1
283	Clinical Science	1
284	Medical (New York)	1
*285	Professional Psychology (Current Title: Professional Psychology: Research and Practice)	1
*286	Annales de Virologie (Current Title: Institut Pasteur. Annales. Virologie.	1
287	Aviation, Space, and Environmental Medicine	1
288	RNABC News (Registered Nurses Association of British Columbia)	1
289	Trans Ophthalmol Soc	1
290	American Journal of Cardiology	1
291	Lijec Vjesn	1
292	Journal of Cutaneous Pathology	1
293	Acta- Dermato- Venereologica	1
294	Nederlands Tijdschrift voor Tandheelkunde	1
295	Sem Hop Paris	1
296	Annals of Clinical Research	1
297	Annales de Pathologie	1
298	Journal of Forensic Sciences	1
299	Biomedicine and Pharmacotherapy	1
300	Kentucky Nurse	1

301	Contact Point	1
302	New York Journal of Dentistry	1
*303	Occupational Health Nursing (Current Title: American Association of Occupational Health Nurses Journal)	1
304	Occupational Health and Safety	1
305	Annales de Medecine Interne	1
306	Revista de Investigacion Clinica	1
307	Boll Ist Sieroter Milan	1
308	Journal of Dental Research	1
309	ASDA News (American Student Dental Association)	1
310	Maryland State Dental Association. Journal	1
*311	Josanpu Zasshi (Current Title: Journal of Intravenous Nursing)	1
312	Journal of Toxicology: Clinical Toxicology	1
*313	NITA (Current Title: Journal of Intravenous Nursing)	1
314	Law, Medicine and Health Care	1
315	International Journal of Psychiatry in Medicine	1
316	Gut	1
317	Hospital Manager	1
318	New Physician	1
319	Weekly Epidemiological Record	1
320	Nursing (83)	1

APPENDIX (continued)

RANK	TITLE OF JOURNAL	NUMBER OF ARTICLES
321	Child Welfare	1
*322	Journal of Medicine (Current Title: Journal of Medicine--Clinical, Experimental, and Theoretical)	1
323	Antimicrobial Agents and Chemotherapy	1
324	Revue Medicale de la Suisse Romande	1
325	Dental Student	1
326	Scandinavian Journal of Immunology	1
327	Community Medicine	1
328	Florida Nurse	1
329	Plastic Surgery News	1
330	Voprosy Virusologii	1
331	Canadian Doctor	1
332	Comp Pathol Bull	1
333	Physician Assistant	1
334	JEMS (Journal of Emergency Medical Services)	1
335	Pathologist	1
336	Journal of Computer Assisted Tomography	1
*337	American Podiatry Association. Journal (Current Title: American Podiatric Medical Association. Journal)	1
338	Annals of Neurology	1
339	AANA Journal (American Association of Nurse Anesthetists)	1
340	Arkansas Medical Society. Journal	1

*341	Hoppe-Seyler's Zeitschrift fuer Physiologische Chemie (Current Title: American Podiatric Medical Association. Journal)	1
342	Fertility and Sterility	1
343	Monatsschrift Kinderheilkunde	1
344	Revue de L'Infirmiere	1
345	Krankenpflege	
*346	Maryland State Medical Journal (Current Title: Maryland Medical Journal)	1
347	Acta Cytologica	1
348	Acta Pathologica, Microbiologica et Immunologica Scandinavica. Section B. Microbiology. Supplementum	1
349	Lamp (Australia)	1
350	International Journal of Dermatology	1
351	Z Gesamte Inn Med	1
352	Gan To Kagaku Ryoho	1
353	Fortschritte Medizin	1
354	American Journal of Psychiatry	1
355	Louisiana State Medical Society. Journal	1
356	Recenti Progressi in Medicina	1
357	New York State Dental Journal	1
358	Kentucky Medical Association. Journal	1
359	Nord Med	1
360	Canadian Dental Association. Journal	1

APPENDIX (continued)

RANK	TITLE OF JOURNAL	NUMBER OF ARTICLES
361	Journal of Clinical Pathology. Supplement	1
362	American Journal of Surgical Pathology	1
363	Arkhiv Patologii	1
364	Ultrastructural Pathology	1
365	Minnesota Medicine	1
366	South Carolina Medical Association. Journal	1
367	Archives of Virology	1
368	Pennsylvania Medicine	1
369	Developments in Biological Standardization	1
370	North Carolina Dental Gazette	1
371	Surgical Neurology	1
372	Archives of Surgery	1
373	Drug Intelligence and Clinical Pharmacy	1
374	Nursing Standard	1
375	Today's OR Nurse	1
376	Med Ideas	1
377	Lyon Med	1
378	Medical Tribune (US)	1
379	British Medical Journal	1
380	Dental Economics	1

381	Journal of Dermatologic Surgery and Oncology		1
*382	Infirmiere Canadienne (Current Title: Canadian Nurse – L'Infirmiere Canadienne)		1
383	Acta Haematologica		1
384	National Medical Association. Journal		1
385	Nursing (Horsham)		1
386	Journal of Laboratory and Clinical Medicine		1
387	Gazette Medicale de France		1
388	UCLA Cancer Center Bulletin		1
389	Revista Clinica Espanola		1
390	Pediatric Infectious Disease Journal		1
391	Cleveland Clinic Journal of Medicine		1
392	Immunological Reviews		1
393	Tidsskr Nor Laegeforen		1
394	Ann Soc Belg Med Trop		1
395	Neurology		1
396	Alabama Journal of Medical Sciences		1
*397	American Journal of Medical Technology		1
398	American Journal of Forensic Medicine and Pathology		1
399	Clinical Obstetrics and Gynecology		1
400	Tissue Antigens		1

APPENDIX (continued)

RANK	TITLE OF JOURNAL	NUMBER OF ARTICLES
401	Journal of Experimental Medicine	1
402	NIPH Annals (National Institute for Public Health)	1
403	Tumori	1
404	Hawaii Medical Journal	1
405	Critical Care Nurse	1
406	Mikrobiyologi Bulteni	1
407	Pennsylvania Nurse	1
408	Medical World News	1
*409	Iowa Medical Society. Journal (Current Title: Iowa Medicine)	1
410	Rinsho Ketsueki	1
411	Lung	1
412	Clinical Chemistry	1
413	Massachusetts Nurse	1
414	Archives of Dermatological Research	1
415	Gastrointestinal Radiology	1
416	American Journal of Dermatopathology	1
417	Thorax	1
418	CA	1
419	Johns Hopkins Medical Journal	1
420	J Med Assoc Ga.	1

SCI TECH COLLECTIONS

Tony Stankus, Editor

Ann Viera presents an outline of the literature on conservation biology, a field which has proved to be of considerable importance.

Brief Guide to Conservation Biology and Its Literature

Ann Viera

SUMMARY. The role of conservation biology in preserving biological diversity and its relationship to older disciplines is described. Information sources are discussed, focusing on developments in the United States over the past ten years. The Appendix lists additional sources.

INTRODUCTION

Time magazine chose the earth as "Planet of the Year" for 1988 instead of choosing a person.[1,2] This ended a year in which the number of articles reported by the news media on global environmental change increased dramatically. Complex environmental problems previously seen as isolated, regional events began to be discussed as interconnected and global. Recognition that the planet is at risk due to ozone depletion, air and water pollution, desertification, and toxic wastes grew as the scientific evidence converged and people across the globe experienced drought, seal epidemics, polluted beaches, and abnormal floods.[3]

William C. Clark, in an introductory article in the September 1989 special issue of *Scientific American* titled "Managing Planet Earth" wrote that "We have entered an era characterized by syndromes of global change that stem from the interdependence between human development and the environment."[4] The issue contained ten articles that examined ". . . the prospects for sustainable human development on a planet with finite resources and a fragile

---

Ann Viera is Assistant Professor and Reference Librarian at the University of Tennessee, Knoxville, TN.

environment."[5] In "Threats to Biodiversity"[6] E.O. Wilson described the widespread habitat fragmentation and destruction that has resulted in an unprecedented number of extinctions. Combined with unstudied synergistic effects of other stresses like pollution or disease, the loss of biological diversity is predicted to increase in the next few decades.[7] Wilson sees the loss of diversity as the most important process of global environmental change. Its effects are irreversible and almost impossible to predict. The focus of this paper is the scientific response to the accelerating loss of biological diversity, the discipline now called conservation biology.

OVERVIEW OF CONSERVATION BIOLOGY

The goal of the Society for Conservation Biology, founded in 1986, is ". . . to help develop the scientific and technical means for the protection, maintenance, and restoration of life on this planet — its species, its ecological and evolutionary processes, and its particular and total environment."[8] Conservation biology is necessarily a mission-oriented or crisis discipline. It integrates both pure and applied aspects of social and biological sciences, as well as philosophy. Michael Soulé, active in both basic research and in articulating the discipline, has explained that "Its [i.e., conservation biology's] relation to biology, particularly ecology, is analogous to that of surgery to physiology and war to political science."[9] Figure 1 shows the various disciplines that comprise conservation biology and juxtaposes it with another crisis discipline, cancer biology.

Conservation biology has been gaining momentum over the past ten years; the events and related publications which account for its current trajectory are listed in Figure 2. Neither the figure nor this overview attempts to document all of the many antecedents of conservation biology. Conservation biology is becoming one of the broadest areas of investigation ever configured, reflecting as it does the scope and complexity of life itself. Soulé believes that the roots of the discipline antedate science.[10] For their practical, theoretical, or philosophical contributions he has identified a diverse group: St. Francis of Assisi, Ashoka, Lao Tzu, Darwin, Elton, Thoreau, Carson, and Leopold, to name a few.[11]

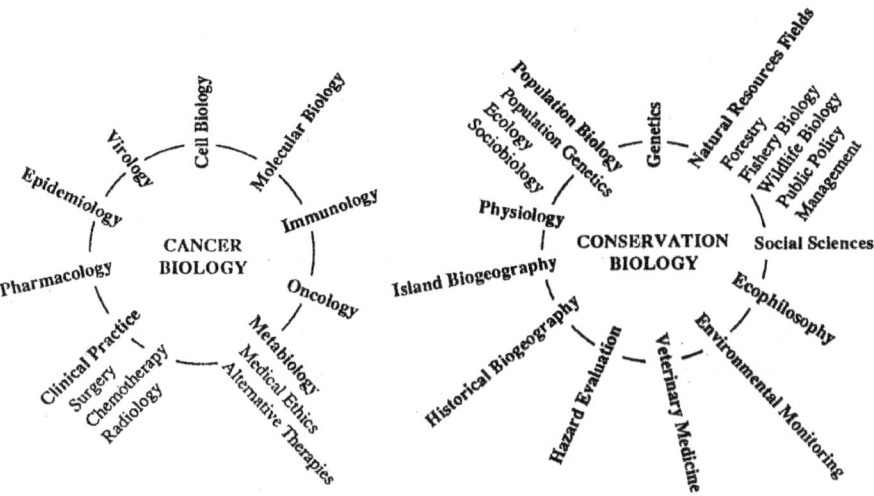

FIGURE 1. Cancer biology and conservation biology are both interdisciplinary sciences. [Adapted, with permission, from Soulé, M. E. 1985. "What is conservation biology?" *BioScience* 36: 727-734. Copyright 1985 by the American Institute of Biological Sciences.]

The unprecedented loss of biological diversity is a direct threat to humans while at the same time it is an often avoidable consequence of human activity. Ironically, much is unknown about what is being lost in terms of the vast library of genetic resources. Donald Falk, Director of the Center for Plant Conservation, described the situation of the loss of genetic resources this way: "do we want to bulldoze the library with all its books inside just as biotechnology is enabling us to decode, read, and use all that information?"[12] Existing information about the abundance and distribution of biological diversity has been described recently as ". . . inadequate, often inaccessible, and frequently inapplicable to conservation management, thus hampering the efficiency of resource policy and management decisions."[13] The rate of extinctions makes the next two decades crucial ones. This paper provides an updated list of sources of information in conservation biology in anticipation of the increasing interest and activity in this area of investigation.

1978   First International Conference on Conservation Biology, University of California, San Diego. Papers published in: Soulé, M.E.; Wilcox, B.A. *Conservation biology: an evolutionary-ecological perspective*. Sunderland, Massachusetts: Sinauer; 1980.

1979   Myers, N. *The sinking ark*. Oxford, England; Pergamon 1979.

1980   IUCN. *World conservation strategy: living resource conservation for sustainable development*. Gland, Switzerland: IUCN; 1980.

1981   Frankel, O.H.; Soulé, M.E. *Conservation and evolution*. Cambridge, Massachusetts: Cambridge University Press; 1981.

1981   Ehrlich, P.R.; Ehrlich, A.H. *Extinction: the causes and consequences of the disappearance of species*. New York: Random House; 1981.

1981   U.S. Department of State. *Proceedings of the U.S. strategy conference on biological diversity*. Washington, D.C.: U.S. Government Printing Office; 1982.

1982   Application of Genetics to the Management of Wild Plant and Animal Populations, Washington, D.C., August 9-13, 1982. Papers published in: Schonewald-Cox, C.M. et al. *Genetics and conservation: a reference for managing wild animal and plant populations*. Menlo Park, California: Benjamin/Cummings; 1983.

1985   Second International Conference on Conservation Biology, University of Michigan, Ann Arbor. Papers published in: Soulé, M.E. *Conservation biology: the science of scarcity and diversity*. Sunderland, Massachusetts: Sinauer; 1986.

1986   Society for Conservation Biology incorporated.

1986   National Forum on Biodiversity, Washington, D.C., September 21-25, 1986. Sponsored by the National Academy of Sciences and the Smithsonian Institution. Papers published in: Wilson, E.O. *Biodiversity*. Washington, D.C.: National Academy Press; 1988.

1987   First issue of *Conservation Biology*, Journal of the Society for Conservation Biology is published.

1988   Research Priorities in Conservation Biology, Marathon, Florida, April 16-18, 1988. Results published in: Soulé, M.E.; Kohm, K.A. *Research priorities for conservation biology*. Washington, D.C.: Island Press; 1989.

1989   Western, D.; Pearl, M.C. *Conservation for the twenty-first century*. New York: Oxford University Press; 1989.

FIGURE 2. Events and Publications in Conservation Biology, A Table Derived from Brussard[14]

SOURCES OF INFORMATION

Guides to the Literature

Davis, E.B. *Using the biological literature: a practical guide*. New York: Marcel Dekker; 1981.

Freeman, R.R.; Smith, M.F. Environmental information. *Annual Review of Information Science and Technology*, 21:241-305; 1986.

Wyatt, H.V. *Information sources in the life sciences*. 3rd ed. London: Butterworths; 1987.

The Butterworths guide is the only one published that treats conservation biology as a separate entity. The chapter on ecology by G.D. Fussey contains a three page section titled "Conservation and Environmental Management" that emphasizes British sources. (This paper offers an expanded list of primarily U.S. sources not covered in general guides like those by Davis, Freeman or Wyatt.)

Bibliographies

These three bibliographies are excellent guides to the ethical and philosophical facets of conservation biology.

Davis, D.E. *Ecophilosophy: a field guide to the literature*. San Pedro, California: R. & E. Miles; 1989.

DeGroh, T. *Deep ecology and environmental ethics: a selected and annotated bibliography of materials published since 1980*. Chicago: Council of Planning Librarians; 1987.

Simmons, D.A. *Environmental ethics: a selected bibliography for the environmental professional*. Chicago: Council of Planning Librarians; 1988.

Library of Congress Subject Headings

CONSERVATION OF NATURAL RESOURCES
WILDLIFE CONSERVATION
PLANT CONSERVATION
NATURE CONSERVATION
BIOLOGICAL DIVERSITY
BIOLOGICAL DIVERSITY CONSERVATION
SPECIES DIVERSITY

Library Call Numbers

LC: QH75-89 Dewey Decimal: 333.7
SK351-579 639.9
GF51-90 301.31
S900-949 363.7
HC79.E5

Journals, Newsletters, and Series

American Naturalist, Biological Conservation, BioScience, BioTropica, Conservation Biology, Evolution, Journal of Tropical Ecology, Nature, and *Science* frequently publish papers about conservation biology. *Ambio, Behavioral Ecology and Sociobiology, Ecology, Environmental Ethics, Forest Ecology, Genetics, Heredity, Journal of Wildlife Management, Oecologia, Oikos, Zoo Biology,* and *Zygon* are some of the other journals publishing pertinent papers.

Newsletters are valuable because they perform a current awareness function in terms of research and bibliographies.[15] *Conservation Biology* and *BioScience,* among others listed above, include useful news sections. The Smithsonian Institution, Department of Botany, National Museum of Natural History, sends its *Biological Conservation Newsletter* to 550 subscribers in 24 countries free of charge. It lists publications and meetings, current literature, educational opportunities and news.

The *Endangered Species Update* monitors developments in the U.S. federal endangered species program and is published by the School of Natural Resources, University of Michigan, Ann Arbor. It includes a reprint of the latest U.S. Fish and Wildlife Service (USFWS) publication *Endangered Species Technical Bulletin,* a feature article, book review, technical notes from the Center for Conservation Biology, Stanford University, and new publications. The USFWS publication was free to anyone who requested it until 1981 and is still distributed to depository libraries. The *Endangered Species Update* ($15/yr U.S.) is recommended for libraries not enrolled in the depository program.

The International Union for Conservation of Nature and Natural Resources (IUCN) publishes the *IUCN Bulletin* quarterly. Indexed by *Biological Abstracts*, it presents a global picture of conservation. Each issue has special reports, book reviews, and new publication announcements.

Intecol Newsletter contains news of the International Association for Ecology (IAE) as well as recent publications. Membership benefits for individuals or libraries/institutions belonging to IAE include large discounts on *Oikos*, *Oecologia*, and 17 other journals.

Resources for the Future provides articles on policy analysis based on its research projects in *Resources*. It is indexed in *PAIS*. News and publications are announced as well. The Conservation Foundation became affiliated with the World Wildlife Fund in 1985. Together they publish three newsletters; all are distributed free of charge. The *Conservation Foundation Letter* focuses on environmental issues and the *World Wildlife Fund Letter* focuses on conservation programs. Resolve is a newsletter which is part of the consensus building/environmental dispute resolution project of the Conservation Foundation. The Conservation Foundation Letter is indexed by six services including *PAIS* and *Environment Abstracts*.

School newsletters like the *Yale Forest School News* from the Yale School of Forestry and Environmental Studies or *Natural Resources News* from the School of Natural Resources, University of Michigan, announce news and publications of their faculty and alumni active in conservation biology. Other newsletters are mentioned elsewhere in this paper.

No single monographic series includes all aspects of conservation biology. Parts of the discipline are covered by series like *Monographs in Population Biology* from Princeton University Press, the *Springer Series on Environmental Management* from Springer-Verlag, and *Population and Community Biology* from Chapman and Hall. Island Press and Sinauer Associates have consistently published books on conservation biology, as have Oxford University Press, Cambridge University Press and University of Chicago Press.

Databases

Many commercially available databases and printed indexes contain bibliographic information of interest to conservation biologists.

They are described in general guides listed above or in directories like the *Cuadra/Elsevier Directory of Online Databases*.

Locating databases not commercially available is more of a challenge. Databases are being created by most of the organizations listed in this paper, often in conjunction with other organizations sharing similar missions, and sometimes to correct perceived shortcomings of existing databases. Biologists at the Center for Conservation Biology at Stanford are developing a Global Species Database (GSD) which will allow a ". . . relatively unbiased and consistent global analysis of threatened species."[16] The Nature Conservancy maintains a Biodiversity Database comprised of data from its global network of reserves.

Data set management in ecological sciences has been recognized as a problem area since 1984.[17] Ecological and biological data tends to be scattered and less standardized than abiotic data[18] and clearinghouses that are supposed to provide information about data files are rarely used and poorly understood.[19] The U.S. Office of Technology Assessment (OTA) found that, (1) maintaining diversity is seldom a goal of the many Federal agencies currently collecting enormous amounts of biological data and, (2) lack of institutional coordination of data collection causes gaps, overlaps in coverage, scattering, and compatibility problems.[20] In 1987 the OTA recommended that a clearinghouse be established for data on biological diversity as part of the effort to enhance the nation's knowledge base. Progress is being made towards that goal. Testimony was heard before a U.S. House of Representatives Subcommittee in May 1989 in support of a National Center for Biological Diversity to be housed in the Smithsonian Institution. The proposed center will function as the clearinghouse for biological diversity data recommended by the OTA.[21] Jonathan Roughgarden of Stanford University recently suggested a more extensive plan, calling for the U.S. Congress to create a U.S. Ecological Survey (USES), analogous to the U.S. Geological Survey. USES would provide neutral descriptive information to the government and the public about ". . . the biological component of the environment and identify processes that shape it."[22] The *Encyclopedia of Information Systems and Services* from Gale Research is the most comprehensive source for locating general information about what databases may exist on a given aspect of conservation biology. Newsletters and direct inquiries of individuals and organizations may be equally useful.

Organizations

International Organizations

The largest international organization involved in strategic planning as well as specific projects is the International Union for Conservation of Nature and Natural Resources (IUCN). Formed in 1948 and active in 117 countries, its 580 members are nations, government agencies, and non-governmental agencies working together on equal terms on conservation problems. Priorities are established every three years by its General Assembly and carried out by its Secretariat and six Commissions. Legal expertise is provided by the IUCN Environmental Law Centre in Bonn, Federal Republic of Germany. The Law Centre is developing or participating in the development of several databases. The IUCN is the scientific and program planning organization for the World Wildlife Fund and works closely with United Nations (U.N.) Environment Programme (UNEP), U.N. Food and Agriculture Organization (FAO), and U.N. Educational, Scientific, and Cultural Organization (UNESCO). IUCN sponsors specialist groups like the African Elephant and Rhino Specialist Group and Captive Breeding Specialist Group. Publications available from the IUCN Conservation Monitoring Centre in Cambridge, U.K. cover threatened species, parks and protected areas, and environmental law and legislation.

The United Nations Environment Programme (UNEP) started the Man and the Biosphere (MAB) Programme in 1971. Through committees in each of its member nations, it commissions studies, by biologists and social scientists, of the human impact on ecosystems and the result of environmental modifications on humans. It has established a network of biosphere reserves throughout the world, and has developed the "Action Plan for Biosphere Reserves" to define a minimum set of activities to be undertaken in each reserve.

Other international organizations include the World Resources Institute, Conservation International, the World Bank and other multilateral development banks, International Council of Scientific Unions/International Geosphere Biosphere Programme, International Council for Bird Preservation, World Health Organization, the World Meteorological Organization, Conservation Foundation/ World Wildlife Fund, and the U.S. Nature Conservancy.

U.S. Government Organizations

U.S. government agencies involved in conservation biology projects include the Smithsonian Institution, National Science Foundation, Environmental Protection Agency, and the U.S. Agency for International Development. To locate detailed information about these and other U.S. government agencies responsible for wildlife conservation policy and programs consult the annual *Audubon Wildlife Report*. Begun in 1985 and averaging 800 pages, it brings together information on agencies and programs: legislation, budget information, and current developments. One agency is featured in a long article each year. Also helpful but broader in scope is the *Conservation Directory* published annually by the National Wildlife Federation.

Foundations

The W. Alton Jones Foundation, Charles A. Lindbergh Fund, MacArthur Foundation, William and Flora Hewlett Foundation, Pew Charitable Trusts, Jessie Smith Noyes Foundation, and the Tides Foundation are some of the U.S. foundations supporting research in conservation biology.

Professional Societies

Many societies are involved with conservation biology on various levels. The main three are the Society for Conservation Biology and two others that are actually federations of societies: American Institute of Biological Sciences (AIBS) and the Association of Systematics Collections (ASC).

Other societies include the Association for Tropical Biology, Society for the Study of Evolution, American Society of Naturalists, National Association of Environmental Professionals, American Association of Zoological Parks and Aquariums, New York Zoological Society/Wildlife Conservation International, Wilderness Society, Chicago Zoological Society, International Association for Ecology, U.S. Academy of Sciences, Soviet Academy of Sciences, American Fern Society, American Ornithologists Union, American

Pharmaceutical Association, American Society of Mammalogists, American Society of Pharmacognosy, American Society of Plant Physiologists, American Society of Plant Taxonomists, American Society of Zoologists, Animal Behavior Society, Association of Field Ornithologists, Botanical Society of America, Ecological Society of America, Society for Ecological Restoration, and the National Audubon Society.

A Brief Directory of Research Centers

Stanford University Center for Conservation Biology, Department of Biological Sciences, Stanford, CA 94305. Paul Ehrlich, President. (415) 723-5924. Founded in 1984 to foster basic and applied research in conservation biology as well as consultation and technical assistance. Publishes news of its activities in *Update*, distributed free of charge.

University of California, San Diego, Project in Conservation Science. Department of Biology C-016, La Jolla, CA 92093. David S. Woodruff, Coordinator. (619) 534-2375. Its purpose is to establish an international center for conservation science research which will facilitate communication between and draw on the people and institutions in San Diego: University of California San Diego, San Diego State University, Hubb Institute/Sea World, and South West Fisheries Research Center.

The Land Institute, 2440 East Water Well Road, Salina, Kansas 67401. Wes and Dana Jackson, Co-directors. Founded 1973. A non-profit educational and research organization devoted to sustainable agriculture and good stewardship of the earth. Internship program for college post-graduates. Results of research published annually in the Land Institute Research Report. Sponsors conferences, annual Prairie Festival, and a grain exchange. A newsletter, *The Land Report*, reviews books as well as reporting on activities of the institute. It is published three times per year; subscription price is $6 (U.S.).

Institute of Ecosystem Studies, New York Botanical Garden, Mary Flagler Cary Arboretum, Box AB, Millbrook, New York 12545. (914)677-5343. Founded in 1983 to promote educational programs in ecology. It is one of the organizations which jointly sponsor the Hubbard Brook Ecosystem Study, begun in 1963 in the

White Mountain National Forest in New Hampshire. Data gathered at Hubbard Brook is rare because of the depth of analysis, consistency, and longevity. A list of publications stemming from research at Hubbard Brook is available upon request.

Center for Plant Conservation, 125 Arbor Way, Jamaica Plain, MA 02130-3520. (617)524-6988. Donald A. Falk, Director. Founded 1984. Coordinates efforts of 19 member consortium to systematically protect, cultivate and study rare and endangered plants. A Newsletter, *Plant Conservation*, is available at no charge.

NOTES

1. Sancton, T.A. What on earth are we doing? *Time*, 133(1):24-73; 1989 January 2.
2. Hoagland, K.E. Global change is key political topic for 1989. *BioScience*, 39(3):151; 1989 March.
3. Worldwatch Institute. *State of the World 1989: a worldwatch institute report on progress toward a sustainable society*. New York: W.W. Norton; 1989.
4. Clark, W.C. Managing planet earth. *Scientific American*. 261(3):47-54; 1989 September.
5. Ibid.
6. Wilson, E.O. Threats to biodiversity. *Scientific American*. 261(3):108-116; 1989 September.
7. Myers, N. Synergistic interactions and the environment. *BioScience*, 39(8):506; 1989 September.
8. Goals and objectives of the Society for Conservation Biology. *Conservation Biology*. 3(1):108; 1989 March.
9. Soulé, M.E. What is conservation biology? *BioScience*. 35(11): 727-734;1985 December.
10. Soulé, M.E. *Conservation biology: the science of scarcity and diversity*. Sunderland, Massachusetts: Sinauer; 1986.
11. Ibid.
12. U.S. Congress. House. *H.R. 1268 – the national biological diversity conservation and environmental research act: hearing before the subcommittee on natural resources, agriculture research and environment of the committee on science, space, and technology*. 101 Congress: 1st Session; 1989 May 17.
13. U.S. Congress. House. *National Biological Diversity Conservation and Environmental Research Act*. 101 Congress, First Session, H.R. 1268.
14. Broussard, P.F. The current status of conservation biology. *Bulletin of the Ecological Society of America*, 66:9-11; 1985.
15. Gilbert, P.; Hamiliton, C.J. *Entomology: a guide to information sources*. London: Mansell; 1983.
16. Sisk, T. Identifying threatened and endangered species: a global analysis

is underway. *UPDATE (Center for Conservation Biology, Stanford University)*, 5(11):6; 1989.

17. Michener, W.K. *Research data management in the ecological sciences*. Columbia, South Carolina: University of South Carolina Press; 1986.

18. Olson, R.J. *Review of existing environmental and natural resource data bases. (ORNL-TM 8928)*. Oak Ridge, Tennessee: Oak Ridge National Laboratory; 1984.

19. Olson, R.J. *Locating machine-readable data files*. Oak Ridge, Tennessee: Oak Ridge National Laboratory; 1983.

20. U.S. Congress. Office of Technology Assessment. *Assessing biological diversity in the United States: background paper #2*. (OTA-BP-F-39). Washington, D.C.: U.S. Government Printing Office; 1986.

21. Blockstein, D.E. U.S. legislative progress toward conserving biological diversity. *Conservation Biology*. 2(4):311-313; 1988 December.

22. Roughgarden, J. The United States needs an ecological survey. *BioScience*. 38(1):5; 1989 January.

APPENDIX

Taken together the books edited by Wilson, Western and Pearl, and the two by Soulé, in Figure 2 provide a comprehensive introduction to conservation biology. Selected additional resources are listed here.

BOOKS — SCIENTIFIC ASPECTS OF CONSERVATION BIOLOGY

Brown, A.H.; Clegg, M.T.; Kahler, A.L.; Weir, B.S. *Plant population genetics, breeding, and genetic resources*. Sunderland, Massachusetts: Sinauer; 1989.

Jordan, W.R.; Gilpin, M.E.; Aber, J.D. *Restoration ecology: a synthetic approach to ecological research*. Cambridge: Cambridge University Press; 1987.

Kim, K.C.; Knutson, L. *Foundations for a national biological survey*. Lawrence, Kansas: Association of Systematics Collections; 1986.

Magurran, A.E. *Ecological diversity and its measurement*. Princeton: Princeton University Press; 1988.

Norton, B.G. *The preservation of species: the value of biological diversity*. Princeton: Princeton University Press; 1986.

Rolston, H. III. *Environmental ethics*. Philadelphia: Temple University Press; 1988.

Soulé, M.E. *Viable populations for conservation*. Cambridge: Cambridge University Press; 1987.

Soulé, M.E. *Evaluation of biodiversity projects*. Washington, D.C.: National Academy Press; 1989.

Usher, M.B. *Wildlife conservation evaluation*. London: Chapman and Hall; 1986.

TEXTBOOKS

Dasmann, R.F. *Environmental conservation*. 5th ed. New York: Wiley; 1984.
Ehrenfeld, D.W. *Biological conservation*. New York: Holt, Rinehart and Winston; 1970.

CONFERENCES

Elliot, H. *Second world conference on national parks.* Yellowstone and Grand Teton National Parks, U.S.A.: International Union for Conservation of Nature and Natural Resources; 1972.
Ehrlich, P.R.; Holdren, J.P. *The cassandra conference: resources and the human predicament*. College Station, Texas: Texas A&M University Press; 1988.
Hall, D.O.; Myers, N.; Margaris, N.S. *Economics of ecosystem management. (Tasks for Vegetation Science, vol. 14)*. Dordrecht: Dr W. Junk; 1985.
Peine, J.D. *Proceedings of the conference on the management of biosphere reserves*. Gatlinburg, Tennessee: U.S. Department of the Interior, National Park Service, Uplands Field Research Laboratory, Great Smoky Mountains National Park; 1985.
UNESCO-UNEP. *Conservation, science and society: contributions to the First international biosphere reserve congress*. Paris: Unesco; 1984.

U.S. GOVERNMENT DOCUMENTS

Fletcher, S.R. et al. Major issue forum: the global environment. *CRS Review*, 10(7):1-27; 1989 August.
Interagency Task Force. *U.S. strategy conference on the conservation of biological diversity: an interagency task force report to congress*. Washington, D.C.: USAID; 1985.
U.S. Congress. Office of Technology Assessment. *Assessing biological diversity in the United States: background paper #2*. (OTA-BP-F-39). Washington, D.C.: U.S. Government Printing Office; 1986.
U.S. Congress. Office of Technology Assessment. *Integrated renewable resource management for U.S. insular areas*. (OTA-F-325). Washington, D.C.: U.S. Government Printing Office; 1987.
U.S. Congress. Office of Technology Assessment. *Technologies to maintain biological diversity*. (OTA-F-330). Washington, D.C.: U.S. Government Printing Office; 1987.

COMPUTER NETWORKS

EcoNet, run by the Institute for Global Communications, provides electronic mail, conferencing, and data bases to many of the organizations mentioned in the guide. For information contact EcoNet at 3228 Sacramento Street, San Francisco, California, 94115. (415) 923-0900.

NON-TECHNICAL SOURCES OF INFORMATION

Ayensu, E.S. (and others). *Our green and living world: the wisdom to save it.* Cambridge: Cambridge University Press; 1984.
Durrell, L. *The state of the ark.* Garden City, New York: Doubleday; 1986.
Ehrlich, A.; Ehrlich P. *Extinction: the causes and consequences of the disappearance of species.* New York: Random House; 1981.
Goldsmith, E.; Hildyard, N. *The earth report: monitoring the battle for our environment.* Los Angeles, California: Price, Stern, Sloan; 1988.
Hoose, P.M. *Building an ark: tools for the preservation of natural diversity through land protection.* Covelo, California: Island Press; 1981.
Jackson, W. *New roots for agriculture.* San Francisco: Friends of the Earth; 1980.
Jacobs, M. *The tropical rain forest: a first encounter.* Berlin: Springer-Verlag; 1988.
Ornstein, R.E.; Ehrlich, P. *New world new mind: moving towards conscious revolution.* New York: Doubleday; 1989.
Tobias, M. *Deep ecology.* San Marcos, California: Avant Books; 1984.
Whitmore, T.C. *Tropical rain forests of the far east.* 2nd ed. Oxford: Clarendon Press; 1984.
World Resources Institute; International Institute for Environment and Development. *World resources 1988-89: a report.* New York: Basic Books; 1988.
Managing Planet Earth. *Scientific American.* 261(3): Special issue; 1989 September.
Planet of the Year: Endangered Earth. *Time.* 133(1); 1989 January.
Gore, R. *Extinctions.* National Geographic, 175(6):662-698; 1989 June.

NEW REFERENCE WORKS IN SCIENCE AND TECHNOLOGY

Arleen N. Somerville, Editor

Reviewers are: Laura Delaney (LD), New York Public Library; Isabel Kaplan (IK), University of Rochester; Kathleen Kehoe (KMK), Columbia University; Donna Lee (DL), University of Vermont; Ellis Mount (EM), Columbia University; Diane J. Reiman (DJR), University of Rochester; Arleen N. Somerville (ANS), University of Rochester; Jack W. Weigel (JWW), University of Michigan.

COMPUTER SCIENCES

Computing information directory: a comprehensive guide to the computing literature. 6th edition. Compiled and edited by Darlene Myers Hildebrandt. Federal Way, WA: Pedaro, Inc., 1989. 410p. $145.00.

The most recent edition of this compilation has some noteworthy changes and enhancements. The first edition was published in 1981 under the title *Computer science resources*. Following the appearance of the second edition in 1985 under the present title, the directory has been revised annually, an important factor, considering the rapid growth of the computing literature. The present edition contains more material in half the number of pages, and the text is more readable, reflecting the advantages of desktop publishing technology. Several chapters make use of modified Key Word in Context (KWIC) indexes to titles, providing additional access to important title words. A Master Subject Index provides further entry points and features subheadings by type of literature.

The directory encompasses a broad scope, including not only the computer science literature but the literature of business and personal computing as well. The first and longest chapter "Computing Journals" lists over 1800 titles, many of them annotated with information of value to librarians building collections or managing serials records. The introductory comments in each chapter tell how to acquire materials, how to use the information in the chapter, and how it relates to the contents of other chapters. One of the most interesting chapters is "Computer Languages," which provides acronyms, full names and at least one citation for over five hundred languages. Noteworthy sections of the Appendix include (A) Association for Computing Machinery (ACM) Special Interest Group (SIG) Proceedings, listed by subject, and (B) Standards Bibliography, new to this edition.

The intended audience for the directory appears to be librarians and information specialists in academic, corporate and large public libraries. Thorough, timely coverage of the computing literature is well worth the price. (DJR)

The 1989 neuro-computing bibliography. 2nd edition. Edited by Casimir C. Klimasauskas. Cambridge, MA: MIT Press; 1989. 624p. $40.00.

Intended to serve as a source book for both beginners and experts in the field of neuro-computing, this revised edition adds 2000 references to the 1500 contained in the 1987 edition. Entries have been prepared, for the most part, from actual copies of the works cited. The editor intended to give a broad overview of the practical applications of neuro-computing as well as a foundation in the basic research that contributed to the development of the discipline. The bibliography draws together scattered references from diverse fields that share connections with neuro-computing.

The source book consists of two sections: an author index and a Key Word in Context (KWIC) index of titles. A helpful feature of the author index is the inclusion of titles with "see" references from secondary to primary authors. The KWIC index can be annoying to use when encountering several pages of listings for commonly used title words such as "model" or "network" or insignificant title words such as "about" and "using." Careful editing would make this section more handy to use. The KWIC index is likely to be more helpful to persons unfamiliar with the field of neuro-computing. The author index can assist researchers and practitioners as they verify or track references.

The next revision of the bibliography should be made available in MS-DOS and Apple Macintosh versions as well as the printed text. For the price, the book is definitely worth buying for academic reference collections and for special libraries in institutions and corporations involved in neuro-computing and related fields such as robotics and computer vision. (DJR)

EARTH SCIENCES

CRC practical handbook of marine science. Edited by Michael J. Kennish. Boca Raton, FL: CRC Press; 1989. 710p. $45.00. ISBN 0-8493-3700-3.

Intended as a reference source for scientists and students of oceanography, this detailed handbook presents selective chemical, physical, and biological data on the marine environment. A variety of topics are addressed including air-sea interactions, marine geology, ocean engineering, and zooplankton. The impact of major discoveries in the field such as seafloor spreading, warm-core rings, and hydrothermal seafloor vents are also considered. Completing the text is an extensive section listing the molecular and structural formulae of organic compounds derived from marine organisms. A subject index and numerous references are provided. Recommended for academic and research collections in oceanography and marine resource management. (LD)

CRC practical handbook of physical properties of rocks and minerals. Edited by Robert S. Carmichael. Boca Raton, FL: CRC Press; 1989. 741p. $45.00. ISBN 0-8493-3703-8.

This detailed handbook is an updated and abridged edition of the multivolume, *CRC Handbook of Physical Properties of Rocks* (1982-1984). With contributions from academic, government, and industry experts, it includes more than 700 pages of tabular and graphical data with a minimum of textual material. Among the many topics covered are densities of rocks and minerals; magnetic properties of rocks and minerals; seismic attenuation; and engineering properties of rock. Abundant references are included as well as a comprehensive subject index. Should prove a useful reference source for academic and research collections in geology, geophysics, materials science, petrophysics, geochemistry, and geotechnical engineering. (LD)

Field geophysics. By John Milsom. New York: Halsted Press; 1989. 182p. $19.95. ISBN 0-470-21156-3. (Geological Society of London Handbook Series)

Describing field techniques and related equipment, this compact guide is directed toward individuals working on small-scale geophysical surveys. Gravity meters, radiometric surveys, resistivity profiling, and detection of seismic waves are among the specific topics addressed. In contrast, surveys likely to be conducted by large field crews such as deep seismic reflection work and marine, airborne and downhole geophysics are not covered. Limited references and a brief subject index complete the text. A useful field guide for working professionals and undergraduates studying geology and geophysics. (LD)

Tide tables 1989, high and low water predictions: central and western Pacific Ocean and Indian Ocean. Riverdale, MD: U.S. Dept. of Commerce, National Oceanic and Atmospheric Administration, National Ocean Service; 1988. 381p. $6.75. ISBN not available.

Tide tables 1989, high and low water predictions: east coast of North and South America including Greenland. Riverdale, MD: U.S. Dept. of Commerce, National Oceanic and Atmospheric Administration, National Ocean Service; 1988. 289p. $6.75. ISBN not available.

Tide tables 1989, high and low water predictions: Europe and west coast of Africa including the Mediterranean Sea. Riverdale, MD: U.S. Dept. of Commerce, National Oceanic and Atmospheric Administration, National Ocean Service; 1988. 204p. $6.75. ISBN not available.

Tide tables 1989, high and low water predictions: west coast of North and South America including the Hawaiian Islands. Riverdale, MD: U.S. Dept. of Commerce, National Oceanic and Atmospheric Administration, National Ocean Service; 1988. 234p. $6.75. ISBN not available.

The National Ocean Service has issued tide tables since 1853 with daily tide predictions beginning in 1867. This edition, published in 4 volumes, supplies daily predictions for 198 reference ports and differences and other constants for approximately 6,000 stations. Each volume also contains a number of additional tables including a table for obtaining the approximate tide height at any time, a table of local mean time of sunrise and sunset for every 5th day of the year for different latitudes, and a table for reducing local mean time to standard time. An index to stations and a glossary of terms are also provided. An excellent reference source for any navigation collection. (LD)

ENGINEERING AND TECHNOLOGY

Aerospace technology centres. London: Longman; 1988. 194p. $245.00. ISBN 0-582-01773-4. Distributed by Gale.

Describes the world's research centers dealing with aeronautics, astronautics, guidance systems, satellite broadcasting and related topics. More than 70 countries are represented; entries are arranged by country, then alphabetically by organization name. Supplementing the usual information is a list of recent activities, an estimate of annual expenditures, and a list of publications issued by the organizations, which include universities, government agencies, research institutes and private companies. There is a subject index and an index of organizational titles. (EM)

Audio engineering handbook. Edited by K. Blair Benson. New York: McGraw-Hill; 1988. 1040p. $79.50. ISBN 0-07-004777-4.

This is a useful reference work on a broad range of topics relating to audible sound and sound reproduction devices. Its 17 chapters cover the physics of sound, perception of sound, sound recording and playback devices (analog disk, digital disk, analog tape, digital tape, etc.), studio production techniques and equipment, audio tests, measurements and standards. Contributors are nearly all from industry. Chapters include bibliographies, graphs, diagrams. Recommended. (IK)

The chemical formulary, v. 28. Editor-in-chief, H. Bennett. New York: Chemical Publishing Company; 1989. 438p. ISBN 0-8206-0328-7.

Another volume in the fascinating series of recipes for the amateur or professional chemist, this volume includes instructions for making cherry pie filling, bath and shower gel, liquid soap, interior semigloss paint, pet stain removal carpet cleaner, fine brass polish, olefinic thermoplastic elastomer, and hundreds of other products. The introduction is delightful to read, with its caveats, instructions, and sample formulations. The Appendix includes a list of trademark chemicals and their suppliers, information on federal laws regulating foods, drugs and cosmetics, a listing of incompatible chemicals, and emergency first aid for chemical injuries. The series is recommended. (IK)

Dictionary of engineering acronyms and abbreviations. By Uwe Erb and Harald Keller. New York: Neal-Schuman Publishers; 1989. 312p. $75.00. ISBN 1-55570-028-4.

The more than 30,000 entries of this work reflect the shorthand terminology of engineering and technology as found in journals, encyclopedias, reference and textbooks. The scope is broad, viz definitions given for "AT": acoustical tile, airtight, ampere turn, antitank, anti-thrombin, audit trail and others, but no reference to the IBM-PC model AT. "VHDL" is given as very high density lipoprotein, but not as VHSIC hardware description language, although VHSIC is defined. The authors note in the introduction that some dictionaries of acronyms and abbreviations are either too general or too specific, others are simply out-of-date. Such flaws may be inherent to this kind of publication, and the work under review is not exempt. (IK)

Directory iron and steel plants. Edited by Dorothy Sukits. Pittsburgh: Association of Iron and Steel Engineers; 1989. 584p. $40.00. ISBN not available.

This directory serves as a concise guide to steelmaking operations in North America and selected overseas nations. Five sections with accompanying geographical indexes list producers of steel and steel-related products. A separate section of suppliers of equipment, products and services is also provided. Other features include the names and addresses of associations and technical organizations in the field as well as a fairly comprehensive list of officers, directors, and committees of the Association of Iron and Steel Engineers. An advertising index and a company name index complete the text. A useful directory for technical and business collections covering the iron and steel industry. (LD)

Encyclopedia of environmental control technology. Volume 2: Air pollution control. Edited by Paul N. Cheremisinoff. Houston: Gulf Publishing; 1989. 1066p. $135.00. ISBN 0-87201-245-X.

The second volume in a series on environmental and industrial pollution control, this book features reviews of the latest research on the control of air pollutants by experts in the fields. Among the topics addressed are source monitoring methods, particle and gas control technology, and transport and diffusion of air pollutants. Computational methods for applying control techniques to air resource management are also considered. Numerous photographs, charts, and diagrams are included as well as extensive references. An up-to-date, detailed reference source for academia and research collections in environmental technology and air pollution control. (LD)

Encyclopedia of environmental control technology. Volume 3: Wastewater treatment technology. Edited by Paul N. Cheremisinoff. Houston: Gulf Publishing; 1989. 684p. $135.00. ISBN 0-87201-247-6.

Addressing the specific problem of wastewater treatment, this volume is the third work in a series on pollution control. The primary foci are wastewater treatment with an emphasis on sludge, and groundwater effects and migration of wastes. Among the specific topics considered are mutagens in the aquatic environment and offsite recycling through waste exchange programs. Chapter references and a subject index are included. A useful reference source for academic and research collections in wastewater treatment and environmental control technology. (LD)

Engineering plastics. Metals Park, OH: ASM International; 1988. 883p. ISBN 0-87170-279-7.

This work has the look and feel of another major reference work produced by ASM International (formerly American Society for Metals), the *Metals Handbook*. Similarly filled with tables, charts, illustrations, graphs, and bibliographies, *Engineering Plastics* is divided into eight sections: general design considerations, guide to engineering plastics families, manufacturing process selection, properties considerations, testing and characterization, materials selection, structural analysis and design, and failure analysis. Authors and chapter reviewers (1:3) are drawn widely from academia and industry.

The Forward notes that the work ". . . represents the first attempt, worldwide, to publish a comprehensive, definitive, exhaustively peer-reviewed handbook of practical information on engineering plastics oriented specifically to engineers in user companies." Herein lies the distinction between *Engineering Plastics* and the *Encyclopedia of Polymer Science* (Wiley, 2d ed., 1985). The former is one volume of text and data targeted for engineering applications. The latter, 16 volumes to date, has broader coverage overall, more detailed information on individual topics, and far more extensive bibliographies.

Recommended. (IK)

Engineers' salaries: special industry report, 1987. Washington, D.C.: Engineering Manpower Commission; 1988. 216p. plus unnumbered appendices. ISBN 0-8716-128-4.

Data for this survey were compiled from responses to questionnaires mailed to EMC's national list of engineering employers. A list of respondents is to be found in the Appendix. Figures reflect base salaries as of February 1, 1987 of 105,738 engineering graduates in 261 private sector companies. Tabular and graphic representations compare engineers' salaries by geographic area, industry (i.e., the chemical industry, construction, aerospace, utilities, etc.), company size, degree level and supervisory responsibility. (IK)

Handbook of ion beam processing technology: Principles, deposition, film modification and synthesis. Edited by Jerome J. Cuomo, Stephen M. Rossnagel and

Harold R. Kaufman. Park Ridge: Noyes Publications; 1989. 438p. $72.00. ISBN 0-8155-1199-X.

This volume is a comprehensive overview of ion beam processing technology, with state-of-the-art chapters written by experts in the field. Major categories cover ion beam technology, sputtering phenomena, film modification and synthesis. Of interest to materials science, surface science (including polymer), thin film researchers. (ANS)

Hazards of optical radiation: A guide to sources, uses and safety. By A. F. McKinlay, F. Harlen and M. J. Whillock. Bristol and Philadelphia: Adam Hilger; 1988. 121p. $48.00. ISBN 0-85274-265-7.

This book is a good guide to sources of optical radiation and their potential hazards. It does not provide safety details needed by workers on-the-job. British standards are emphasized. With the current extensive use of lasers, readers concerned about safety would be better served by *Laser Safety Guide* (Laser Institute of America, 6th edition, 1987), *Practical Laser Safety* (D.C. Winburn, Dekker, 1985), and *Laser Safety Training Manual* (Rockwell Associates, Cincinnati, 6th edition, 1983). (ANS)

Properties of amorphous silicon. 2nd ed. (EMIS Datareviews Series No. 1) London and New York: INSPEC, The Institution of Electrical Engineers; 1989. 649p. $260.00 ISBN 0-95296-480-3.

This completely rewritten and updated version of the 1985 edition summarizes information required by new researchers in fields using amorphous silicon. Each chapter describes specific properties, such as density and spin density, conductivity, optical energy gap, optical functions, infrared spectra, visible light spectra, photoluminescence, photoconductivity, mechanical and thermal properties, film growth, and superlattices of the most important amorphous silicon structures. Chapters are written by invited authors or EMIS staff (the Information Services staff of INSPEC) and include extensive bibliographies. (ANS)

What every chemical technologist wants to know about . . . Volume III: plasticizers, stabilizers and thickeners. Compiled by Michael and Irene Ash. New York: Chemical Publishing Co., Inc.; 1989. 412p. $180. ISBN 0-8206-0329-5.

The bulk of this four hundred page book contains hard to find information about plasticizers, stabilizers and thickeners. For each substance, the following information is provided: synonyms, tradename equivalents, Chemical Abstracts Services Registry Numbers, molecular formula, structure, properties, applications, and storage and handling. The property values vary by substance and generally include: form, color, odor, solubility, specific gravity, density, viscosity, melting point, and boiling point. Other properties are listed when relevant to these applications, such as flash point, pour point, saponification number, solidification point, and cloud point. Indexes by tradename and generic synonyms and location of substances. Recommended. (ANS)

HEALTH SCIENCES

ABMS annual report and reference handbook—1989. Evanston, IL: American Board of Medical Specialties; 1989. 103p. $3. ISBN not given.

The report describes the ABMS membership, governance, policies, and programs. Only 23 different medical specialties are officially recognized by the ABMS, though other "specialties" can be found listed in phone books and other forms of advertising. While this publication would be most appropriate for medical libraries, public library patrons seeking to evaluate their physicians' credentials might also find the book helpful. (DL)

The American Medical Association encyclopedia of medicine. Edited by Charles B. Clayman. New York: Random House; 1989. 1184p. $39.95. ISBN 0-394-56528-2.

A number of medical guides for the layperson have been published because patients want to be informed about their own care, are intelligent enough to understand a clear explanation, and can't always get that information from their own physician. The AMA has finally come to terms with these facts and has published their own layperson's guide. The book attempts to cover a broad range of health care and biological topics, but not in any great detail. The person who has just developed Trigeminal Neuralgia, for instance, would certainly want to know more than can be found here. First aid topics are also not described thoroughly. In fact, the book might be best thought of as a good, complete dictionary, rather than an encyclopedia. Readers would want to have it on hand while they read through medical or nursing textbooks. Definitions are clear and enhanced by plentiful line drawings and photographs. The volume is of excellent quality, but would serve best as an adjunct to other health care sources. (DL)

Association of academic health centers 1989 directory. Washington, D.C.: Association of Academic Health Centers; 1989. 133p. $10. ISSN 0276-6590.

Created to coordinate cooperation between US and Canadian academic health centers, this organization now has over 100 members. Eligible academic health centers are those with a school of medicine and at least one other health related, degree granting program such as nursing, veterinary medicine, allied health, dentistry, PhD programs, pharmacy, or public health. The directory lists each member's address, phone number, programs, affiliated hospitals, deans, and other senior staff. (DL)

The Complete grants sourcebook for nursing and health. By David G. Bauer and the American Association of Colleges of Nursing. Edited by Barbara K. Redman. New York: American Council on Education and Macmillan Publishing; 1988. 298p. $49.95. ISBN 0-02-925901-0.

The bulk of the directory lists foundations, corporations, and federal agencies which provide grants to nursing professionals. Brief entries for each organization outline areas of interest, amounts of money given, eligibility, officers, application processes, some former recipients, and analyses. Indexes by activities funded, subjects of interest, and geographical location aid access. While the author has taken much of his information from other publications, some additional sources, thorough verification of each entry, and the nursing focus make this guide most useful for hospital libraries where nurses don't have the time to investigate all of the other publications available. (DL)

Freelance directory of medical communication services. Bethesda, MD: American Medical Writers Association; 1989. 96p. $10. ISBN not given.

This reference describes about 300 freelancers by listing the services they will provide, the subjects they're willing to cover, the media they work in, the books or journals they've worked with, and any other communications credits. Entries are arranged by name. Geographic, service, and subject indexes provide access. Subjects range from recognizably medical topics to related topics like anthropology and artificial intelligence. Services include editing and proofreading, audiovisual production, consumer education, and marketing. (DL)

Health legislative issues. Chicago: AMA Division of Legislative Activities; 1989. 81p. Free. No ISBN given.

The American Medical Association has taken stands on a number of health related political issues. The 1989 edition of this annual publication covers forty-five current political concerns, from Animals in Biomedical Research to Firearms to Smoking. In two or three pages per topic the authors review the medical and political history of each issue, and describe the AMA's stance. Matters under discussion in both federal and state governments are covered and include, for example, AIDS, catastrophic coverage, animals in biomedical research, long-care financing, twelve aspects of Medicare, Medicaid, quality of care, anabolic steroids, smoking and several tobacco concerns. Interestingly, abortion does not appear as either a state or federal issue. (DL)

The Hospital phone book. Miami, FL: US Directory Service; 1989. 264p. $43.95. ISBN 0-916524-34-5.

US hospitals are listed by state and city. The only information given for each hospital is its address and phone number. An index provides access by hospital name. Though this directory contains considerably less information than the *AHA Guide to the Health Care Field*, it is much cheaper and easier to use if all you need is a hospital's name, location, or phone number. (DL)

National guide to foundation funding in health. Edited by John Clinton. New York: The Foundation Center; 1988. 603p. $104.95. No ISBN given.

United States national, regional, and local foundations with a focus on health care and assets of over $1 million are described in this directory. For each of the 2,599 foundations summarized, the guide lists the address, date of establishment, donors, financial data, activities, officers, and application information. Since only those organizations which have expressed a specific interest in health issues are included, fund seekers may want to explore additional sources listing organizations with more general interests. (DL)

LIFE SCIENCES

Dictionary of immunology. Fred S. Rosen, Lisa A. Steiner and Emil R. Unanue. New York, NY: Stockton Press; London: MacMillan Press; 1989. 223p. ISBN 0-333-34742-0. $50.00.

This is the best immunology dictionary that is currently available. It is suitable for biology and health sciences students, researchers, and clinicians. The authors have included terminology from molecular biology, genetics, and cell biology, as well as from immunology proper. The definitions of major concepts, biological structures, and biochemical processes are extensive—many are as long as encyclopedia articles. The definitions are well written and some include tables, flowcharts, diagrams or graphs which clarify the text. The dictionary is an excellent reference tool for biology and health sciences collections. (KMK)

Dictionary of plant pathology. By Paul Holliday. New York: Cambridge University Press; 1989. 369p. $55.00. ISBN 0-521-3317-X.

This is an excellent dictionary which contains a wealth of bibliographic information on plant pathology. The volume includes over 8000 entries of species of fungi, bacteria, viruses, mollicutes, nematodes and viroids which are pathogenic to plants. There are also entries for major crops and plant diseases, pesticides, and agricultural terms. The entries include descriptions of the organism, plant, or disease and one or more current citations to the relevant literature. The author has included brief biographies of prominent plant pathologists. He has also provided a list of the major texts which are important to this area of research. The dictionary is highly recommended for Agriculture and Biology collections. (KMK)

Glossary of plant tissue culture. By Danielle J. Donnelly and William E. Vidaver. Portland, Oregon: Dioscorides Press, 1988. 141p. (Advances in plant science series; vol. 3.). ISBN 0-931146-12-7. Price $17.50.

This glossary's purpose is to provide an aid to the interpretation of the plant culture literature. It contains brief definitions of cell structures, concepts, methodological terms, reagents, concepts, chemical names, and equipment names. There are also personal entries which provide a brief statement of the researcher's major contributions. The personal name entries are limited in their usefulness because they do not provide any biographical data on the subjects. Plant species names are not included in the book. This dictionary will be useful to researchers from other areas of biological research and to students of biology and agriculture. (KMK)

RMS dictionary of light microscopy. Compiled by the Nomenclature Committee of the Royal Microscopical Society. By S. Bradbury et al. New York: Oxford University Press; 1989. (Royal Microscopical Society handbooks; 15.) 139p. ISBN 0-19-856421 (hardback) 0-19856413-9 (pbk.) $10.50.

This slender volume is a specialized dictionary limited to the words used in the literature of light microscopy. The dictionary was compiled by a Royal Microscopical Society (RMS) committee in an effort to standardize the terminology of the subdiscipline. There are approximately 1250 entries which include methodological terms, salient concepts, the names of equipment and chemical reagents, and relevant optical terms. The definitions are brief. Synonyms and abbreviations are cross referenced to the primary entries. There are three appendices which provide French and German translations of the dictionary's terms. The volume's narrow scope limits its usefulness to medical libraries and biology libraries. (KMK)

Virology: directory and dictionary of animal, bacterial and plant viruses. By Roger Hull, Fred Brown and Chris Payne. New York: Stockton Press; 1989. 325p. $79.00. ISBN 0-333-39063-0.

This dictionary includes all the viral species which have been classified by the International Committee on the Taxonomy of Viruses (ICTV) to date. Thus it encompasses bacterial, plant, invertebrate, and vertebrate viruses. In addition to the viruses' names, the entries include methodological terms, reagents, formulae, facts, hypotheses, and salient concepts in virology. The entries vary in length from a few lines up to 250 words. Some of the longer definitions include tables and/or diagrams to illustrate the text. All of the viral species entries include taxonomic information, structural information, the names of the species host(s), and a reference for further reading. The volume is extensively cross referenced. The authors included 7 appendices; six are lists of insects which are infected by particular viruses. The seventh appendix is a list of the properties of phage isolate. This is a useful dictionary for Biology, Agriculture or Medical library collections. (KMK)

PHYSICAL SCIENCES

CODATA key values for thermodynamics. Edited by J.D. Cox, D.D. Wagman, V.A. Medvedev. New York: Hemisphere Publishing Corp.; 1989. 285p. $59.50. ISBN 0-89116-758-7.

This is the final report of the CODATA Task Group on Key Values for Thermodynamics. It presents the basic thermodynamic properties of 151 key chemical elements, aqueous ions, and substances, describes the evaluation process, and provides an extensive bibliography. Important for thermodynamics researchers. (ANS)

Determination and use of stability constants. By Arthur E. Martell and Ramunas J. Motekaitis. New York: VCH Publishers Inc.; 1988. 216p. $35.00. ISBN 0-89573-741-8.

This is a comprehensive treatment which discusses stability constants calculations by a well-known expert, Arthur Martell. The book includes a thorough description of the experimental requirements needed to obtain high quality experimental data and to explain, in detail, computational methods for determining stability constants from such data. Included with the book are three Fortran 77 computer programs on a 5 1/4" MS DOS diskette. Recommended for all research chemistry collections. (ANS)

Purification of laboratory chemicals. 3rd ed. Edited by D.D. Perrin and W.L.F. Armarego. Oxford: Pergamon Press; 1988. 500p. $75.00 hardcover. $37.50 flexicover. ISBN 0-08-034715-0 (hardcover) ISBN 0-08-034714-2 (flexicover).

This third edition updates and expands a 1980 reference source relied on by bench chemists. The core chapter provides brief descriptions for purifying approximately 4000 organic chemicals, while another chapter covers purification methods for 750 inorganic and organometallic substances. Entries range from one line to one page for the most common solvents, such as methanol and benzene. A new chapter describes purification techniques for 100 biological substances. Toxicity data for relevant compounds has been added. The Chemical Abstracts Service Registry Numbers are now listed for each substance for the first time. Practical, concise descriptions are provided for such common techniques as distillation, crystallization, drying, and chromatography, as well as general methods for purifying classes of compounds, such as aldehydes, ketones, phenals, and nitriles. A selected bibliography, unfortunately dated, lists major books on chemical laboratory safety and the major purification methods. Recommended for all chemistry collections. (ANS)

Uranometria 2000.0. By Wil Tirion, Barry Rappaport, and George Lovi. Richmond, Virginia: Willmann-Bell; 1987-88. 2 v. $39.95 each. ISBN 0-943396-14-X (v. 1). ISBN 0-993396-15-8 (v. 2).

This new astronomical atlas shows all stars in the northern and southern hemispheres of the sky down to magnitude 9.5, thus covering well over 300,000 stars in all. Thousands of non-stellar objects—galaxies, nebulae, quasars, etc.—are also included. As the title suggests, the positions of all objects have been specified as of January 1, 2000. The large number of charts (435) has made it possible to use a relatively large scale without resorting to inordinately large pages. As is true for many of the best terrestrial atlases, the edge of each chart overlaps in coverage with the edges of the adjoining charts. The charts are very clear and have a refreshingly uncluttered appearance, and the two-volume set constitutes a very practical tool for amateur and professional astronomers alike. The computerized set of data on which the present atlas is based will also be used to generate a future three-volume set tentatively entitled *Uranometria 2000.0 Star Catalog.* In the meantime, the atlas is highly recommended both for academic and public libraries. (JWW)

SCIENCE, GENERAL

American men & women of science 1989-90: a biographical directory of today's leaders in physical, biological and related sciences. 17th ed. Edited by Basil

Daley, Jim Olsson and Edgar Adcock. New York: R.R. Bowker; 1989. 7775p. in 8 volumes. $650.00 (set). ISBN 0-8352-2568-2 (set).

The latest edition of this standard reference work provides biographical sketches on more than 125,000 active U.S. and Canadian scientists working in over 164 subspecialties. Approximately 65% of the entries are either new or revised with almost 4,000 entries appearing for the first time. As in past editions, entries are arranged alphabetically by scientists' last names and include such information as birthdate, birthplace, degrees earned, professional experience, research specialties, honors, awards, mailing address, etc. A separate Discipline Index listing entrants alphabetically by specialty provides an additional access point. A truly indispensable directory for science collections of all levels. (LD)

Encyclopedia of Associations. International Organizations. 23d ed. Detroit: Gale Research, Inc.; 1989. 2 vols. $390.00 (incl. supplement). ISSN 1041-0023.

In this edition the scope is enlarged to include nonprofit organizations that are international in scope with headquarters outside the U.S., regardless of whether they were national, binational or multinational. Previously only multinational organizations were listed. Also, for the first time are 1,000 multinational associations headquartered in the U.S. that were formerly listed only in the National Organizations volume. Altogether there are now more than 8,000 associations listed in this set; a supplement is issued annually. Organizations are arranged by broad categories. It is interesting to note that there were over 1,000 organizations listed in the sci-tech category and nearly 900 in the health and medical grouping. The usual information is listed for each organization; there are indexes arranged by name/keyword, names of executives and geographical location. (EM)

European sources of scientific and technical information. 8th ed. London: Longman; 1989. 375p. $215.00. ISBN 0-582-03379-9. Distributed by Gale.

Serves as a useful guide to key sources of scientific and technical information found in the countries of Western and Eastern Europe. Seems very wide in its array of countries, despite the absence of the USSR. Organizations discussed include universities, institutes, technical libraries, government departments, museums and trade associations. There are 25 chapters, primarily arranged by disciplines, such as agriculture, engineering, health and safety, metallurgy and the like. Besides the usual directory information, entries indicate the subject fields in which involved information services (translations, search techniques, etc.), library collection strengths and publications issued. Has a subject index as well as one arranged by titles of organizations listed. (EM)

Rules of thumb for physical scientists. Compiled by David J. Fisher. Brookfield: Trans Tech Publications; 1988. 320p. $65.00. ISBN 0-87849-524-X.

Concise, brief definitions for rules-of-thumb from the physical sciences literature are found in this interesting book. Definitions are written for scientists. Terms that have been coined as long ago as 1842 or as recently as 1987 are included. While other rule-of-thumb books exist, none focus on science. Potential interest in large physical science collections. (ANS)

Science and technology annual reference review, 1989. Edited by H. Robert Malinowsky. Phoenix: Oryx Press; 1989. 236p. $55.00. ISBN 0-89774-487-X.

The 1st edition of this annual publication reviews over 600 current and classic sci/tech reference books of all levels. Titles in this issue were drawn from a wide variety of scientific and technical fields including agriculture, astronomy, biology, chemistry, computer science, earth science, general science, mathematics, medicine, physics, and technology. Within each subject area, entries are arranged alphabetically by type of publication (e.g., bibliographies, dictionaries, directories, etc.). Most reviews are several paragraphs in length and contain a general description of the book, a comparison with similar sources, a discussion of the item's good and bad points, and a purchase recommendation. Four useful indexes—title, name, subject, and type of library—provide quick and easy access to reviews. Recommended for sci/tech libraries of all levels. (LD)

Technical writing for industry. By Larry A. Riney. Englewood Cliffs; Prentice Hall; 1989. 288 p. $23.00. ISBN 0-13-901828-X.

This book discusses the fundamentals for writing clearly and concisely, as well as writing for technical applications. It will enormously help industrial technical writers survive in any type of technical writing program. Initial chapters cover: knowing your audience; following ten basic writing guidelines; following guidelines for effective technical writing; and communicating with artwork. Technical examples are used throughout these basic chapters. Several chapters focus on writing useable technical operation instructions. No index; detailed table-of-contents serves as an index. Recommended for all collections that serve technical writers. (ANS)

SCI-TECH ONLINE

Ellen Nagle, Editor

DATABASE NEWS

Beilstein Online

The electronic version of the *Beilstein Handbook of Organic Chemistry*, is now available on DIALOG. The *Handbook*, produced by the Beilstein Institute in Frankfurt, West Germany, is considered the single largest collection of critically reviewed factual data for organic compounds. *Beilstein*, which consists of over 350 volumes dating back to 1779, contains substance information, chemical reactions, physical properties, chemical data, general information, and bibliographic references to the primary chemical literature. The Beilstein Institute reviews and evaluates information from more than 2,000 journals, monographs, and patents for inclusion in the *Handbook*.

Beilstein Online represents the conversion of the *Handbook* and its five supplementary series of volumes into machine-readable form. The online version brings together in a single record all of the information that is available on a chemical substance from the main work and any of the supplements. It enables chemical searching without assuming prior knowledge of the Beilstein indexing system. Initially, *Beilstein Online* includes heterocyclic and acyclic compounds corresponding to volumes 17-27 and 1-4 of the *Handbook*, which covers literature published from 1779 to 1959 plus unreviewed data for heterocycles from literature published from 1960 to 1979. The database will be updated several times a year until the complete file is loaded by the early 1990s.

The database is composed of two parts: the factual file of information associated with specific organic substances and the structural file of the graphic structures of these substances. The factual file contains records for over 1.7 million substances. Each substance record includes the Beilstein Registry Number, the substance name in English and German, formula weight, and molecular formula. Records also include data and references to: substance identification, synthesis and reactions, structure and energy parameters, states of aggregation, mechanical properties, thermodynamic data, transport phenomena, optical and spectral data, magnetic and electrical data, electrochemical behavior, and multicomponent systems data.

Beilstein Online is the first database to use a new DIALOG graphic structure searching capability. Structure searching is based on the ROSDAL (Representation of Organic Structure Descriptions Arranged Linearly) structure language. ROSDAL is an alphanumeric translation of chemical structures which is used to represent both query input and results. It can be used without using a graphics program, or with DIALOGLINK and MOLKICK software.

Searchers can do full structure, substructure, or generic substructure queries on the database. *Beilstein Online*, available as File 390, costs $3.67 per connect minute. Structure output is priced at $1.60 to $2.25 per representation. The price for printing a record is $9.60 plus structure charge. Structure charges range from an additional $9.70 for a structure search to $49 for a substructure search. Since records on this full text database can range from a single item to 250 pages of data, DIALOG provides two free display formats to assist the searcher in evaluating search results.

Polymer Online Introduced

Polymer Online can now be searched on DIALOG as File 322. The database is the online version of the *Encyclopedia of Polymer Science and Engineering*, second edition. The file provides comprehensive coverage of polymer science and engineering, including materials, methods, and the latest advances in macromolecular science. Natural and synthetic polymers, plastics, fibers, elastomers, and processing are all included in the scope of the database. Complete coverage is provided for synthetic and natural polymeric materials; polymer properties (molecular, physical, mechanical, biological, morphology, compatibility); methods, processes, equipment (physical processes, synthesis and reactions, characterization methods, engineering processing, test methods); uses; and general background and definitions.

The online file provides many additional access points than the print equivalent, including indexing of all tables and the complete text of each article. Records include bibliographic information, an abstract, summary information, section headings, tables, figure titles, and descriptors. The database, which contains 18,000 records, will be updated as supplements and revisions are made available. Search costs are $1.42 per search minute; $.25 for each record printed online; $.55 for records printed offline.

AIDS Databases Announced

The National Library of Medicine (NLM) has added two new databases to make information about clinical trials available to persons infected with HIV, health care providers, researchers, and others. A specific directive of the Health Omnibus Programs Extension Act of 1988 (Public Law 100-607) provides that certain information about AIDS-related clinical trials be made public through a database. In response to this, NLM is offering *AIDSTRIALS* and *AIDSDRUGS*.

AIDSTRIALS (*AIDS Clinical Trials*) contains information about clinical trials of agents undergoing evaluation for use against AIDS and related diseases. Included in the database are the title of the trial, trial purpose, agent being studied, trial phase, diseases studied, patient inclusion and exclusion criteria, locations at which the study is taking place, and whether the trial is still open (adding patients to the study). Information comes from two sources. The National Institute of Allergy and Infectious Diseases (NIAID) is providing detailed information about all AIDS-related clinical trials funded by the National Institutes of Health (NIH). The FDA is providing information about non-NIH funded clinical trials studying efficacy.

The companion database, *AIDSDRUGS*, contains descriptive information about the agents being tested in clinical trials. As new trials are added to *AIDSTRIALS*, information will be compiled about the agents and added to *AIDSDRUGS*. The description includes synonyms for the name of the agent including trade names, the standard chemical name, pharmacology, contraindications, adverse reactions, manufacturer, and physical/chemical properties such as molecular composition, molecular formula, and molecular weight. The information contained in both databases is also available through the AIDS Clinical Trials Information Service (1-800-TRIALSA), a telephone hotline staffed by health and information professionals. The hotline will provide information to the general public as well as health professionals. The free service is a Public Health Service project sponsored by NIAID and FDA, in cooperation with the Centers for Disease Control.

World Translations Database Available

A source for translations of literature from all languages in all fields of science and technology is now offered online. *World Translations Index (WTI)* contains translations announcements from the joint database producers, the International Translations Centre (ITC) of the Netherlands and the Centre National de la Recherche Scientifique/Institut de l'Information Scientifique et Technique (CNRS/INIST) of France. The file contains references to both the original and the translated documents. Particular subject emphasis is given to the fields of materials (e.g., metals, plastics, ceramics) and mechanical, industrial, civil and marine engineering. Other heavy subject concentrations include the biomedical and medical sciences and chemistry. Also included are translations relating to earth sciences, oceanography, agriculture, physics, and electronics and electrical engineering. Translations cited are in Western languages; nearly 70 percent are for translations into English. Of these, Russian-to-English translations account for almost 50 percent; German- and Japanese-to-English translations each account for fifteen percent.

The database corresponds to the print publication *World Translations Index* and contains citations to both serial and nonserial publications, including conference proceedings, maps, monographs, patents, reports, standards, technical handbooks, and theses. The initial database contains 160,000 records from 1984 to the present. There are monthly updates; a backfile to 1979 will be added later. Information is provided for obtaining copies of translations. Eventually, online ordering via DIALOG will be available. File 295 costs $1.60 per connect minute. Citations printed online or offline cost $1.75 each.

SCI-TECH IN REVIEW

Karla J. Pearce, Editor

LIBRARIES AND "THE TWO CULTURES"

Budd, John M. Research in the two cultures: the nature of scholarship in science and humanities. *Collection Management*. 11(3/4): 1-20; 1989.

In 1959, C.P. Snow described the difference between the cultures of science and of the humanities. The author of this article applies these differences to the manner in which scientists and humanists conduct their bibliographic research. After the obligatory discussion of the difficulties scientists and humanists experience when they communicate with each other, he comments on how differently they "conduct their business." Scientists work with the concrete, using and establishing paradigms "which, employed as models or examples can replace explicit rules as a basis for the solution of the remaining puzzles of normal science." For those in the humanities, on the other hand, problems "center on the products of man's imagination, on ideas, on these matters for which no rules exist." Scientific knowledge is cumulative or "diachronic" (Snow's definition) while knowledge in the humanities is produced from the individual and subjective perspective of the scholar. He extrapolates these research goals to the way that scholars use the library, consult the literature and cite previous research. While this raises some interesting points, I seriously question the extent to which the author applies C.P. Snow's theories, as well as his own understanding of the nature of scientific research. (KJP)

LIBRARY PERSONALITIES YOU MIGHT KNOW

Crawford, Walt. The trailing edge: gurus, guides and ghosts. *Library Hi Tech*. 7(2): 91-101; 1989.

There are two types of library microcomputer consultants. One, a "guru," provides the answers or results that are requested without taking his or her clients through the reasoning that led up to that decision. A "guide," on the other hand, works with the library staff from the start, making sure that they understand all that went into his or her final decision. The guide's approach is best for most microcomputer projects: deciding when and for what purpose to buy computers, which software is better for a library's particular needs, and for setting up training programs for software use. Only when customized database applications are needed, will the guru's approach be as useful. Situations where a library can profit from the advice of a consultant are described, as well as how to choose the right one. The author also discusses vaporware, or "ghosts," and how to keep from being fooled by its false promises. (KJP)

THE ELECTRONIC LIBRARY—NOW?

Kibbey, Mark; Evans, Nancy J. The network is the library. *Educom Review*. 24(3): 15-20; 1989 Fall.

The electronic library, defined here as a "network of information tools and services," will soon be here. Information access points in institutions such as Carnegie-Mellon in Pittsburgh, are being connected through electronic networks. Publishers are making available more and more information that is in machine-readable form. With an electronic network, users do not need to know whether the information they need is held locally or in an information center many miles away. A query from their workstation will give researchers access to whatever database will provide their needed answers. Access will be to full text word and datasets, that will call for no special expertise to use. Project Mercury at Carnegie-Mellon is a pilot project to test the feasibility of this vision for the future. (KJP)

NATIONAL RESEARCH NETWORK

Lynch, Clifford A. Library automation and the national research network. *Educom Review*. 24(3): 21-26; 1989 Fall.

Building on the use of national utilities (OCLC, RLIN) for cataloging, libraries are moving towards the development of a national research network. Having become accustomed to the increased power of online catalog searches—it is now possible, for example, for the users of MELVYL at the University of California to obtain, with one command, a list of the library's 127 seventeenth-century publications in Portuguese—users expect more from their library service. And they also have access to article level information through MEDLINE in the library catalog. These new capabilities bring up questions that must be addressed: how do we handle copyright for non-print materials; how do we separate the user interface from the retrieval system; how do we decide among information networks; and how can we provide academic and economic support for their use? In the 1990s, information technologies will change substantially how we conduct our research. (KJP)

SERIALS INFLATION—A BRITISH PERSPECTIVE

Merriman, John B. Publishing and perishing. *Nature*. 341: 349-350; 28 September 1989.

While library budgets are shrinking, more journals are being produced. The author, a Director with B.H. Blackwell in England, cites some of the reasons for the journal problems of the 1980s. Spending on published materials in British universities in the decade between 1978 and 1987 has declined 25% in real terms. In Canada, over the past ten years, librarians have canceled 40,000 subscriptions, with a value of $4.2 million. This happened while numbers of titles were increasing; in 1987, for example, by 12%.

The publishers are not the only ones responsible for this, since scientists are producing more and needing to publish more. His remedies, unfortunately, are not radical—more careful attention by librarians to ratios of price versus usage for individual titles, and encouraging scholars not to serve on editorial boards of journals with unreasonable pricing policies. A useful table and figures are included. (KJP)

DUPLICATING JOURNAL SUBSCRIPTIONS

Stubbe, Lisa Aren. Characteristics of serials duplication within an academic research library. *Library and Information Science Research.* 11(2): 91-108; 1989 April-June.

With the University of Michigan as a model, the author characterizes serials duplication among university departmental libraries. Using a sample taken from their almost 18,000 current periodical and annual subscriptions, she hypothesized that 10% of them would be duplicated and that the costs of duplicates would comprise no more than 25% of the serials budget. These titles would also be more expensive and be more likely to be held in the more discipline-related divisional libraries, in particular, the science libraries. In her results she found that 17% of the sample were duplicates, and that their average price was over 60% greater than those for which single subscriptions were held, although the duplicate subscriptions' average price was inflated by a very few, very expensive titles. The largest area of duplication—21%—was indeed in the sciences. She also found that the titles duplicated were most likely to have started in the period between the end of World War II and 1975. An interesting and very readable research report. (KJP)

ENCOURAGING INNOVATION

Webb, T.D.; Jensen, Edward A. Managing innovative information technology. *Journal of Library Automation.* 10(2/3); 131-142; 1989.

From a special issue devoted to "Creativity, Innovation, and Entrepreneurship in Libraries," the authors link our librarians' belief in the people's right to information and our respect for the power of human reason to successful managerial techniques. Library managers can apply that philosophy to encourage innovation by developing "an atmosphere of choice and freedom with minimal rules and policies." The sort of managerial environment that inspires creativity is described, as well as the characteristics of a creative employee. Employees should not be penalized for failures and setbacks, for instance, since they allow one to gain more information about the task and about oneself. By encouraging adaptability, creativity and commitment in the staff, a library manager will help them and the organization to grow and adapt to change while becoming more productive. (KJP)

For Product Safety Concerns and Information please contact our EU representative GPSR@taylorandfrancis.com
Taylor & Francis Verlag GmbH, Kaufingerstraße 24, 80331 München, Germany

www.ingramcontent.com/pod-product-compliance
Lightning Source LLC
Chambersburg PA
CBHW052130300426
44116CB00010B/1849